Wonderful Ways
With Food

by Margaret Deeds Murphy

Dorison House Publishers
Boston

About the Author

Margaret Deeds Murphy, author and Home Economist, was born in Stromsburg, Nebraska, received her Home Economics degree from the University of Nebraska in 1937, and has been cooking, testing and writing about food ever since. She is the author of a number of cookbooks, has been associated with several national magazines, was head of the Recipe Test Kitchens at General Foods Corporation as well as having her own consulting practice in New York City.

Maggie, as she is known to her friends, lives with her husband on Cape Cod where she operates a test kitchen for the development of recipes and does food writing. She has prepared food pages for Gray's Sporting Journal and writes a weekly food column for the Cape Cod Oracle of Orleans, Massachusetts.

Acknowledgments

The author wishes to thank the following people at West Bend for their encouragement and assistance:

Joanne Turchany: Manager, Consumer Information
Barbara Drabowicz: Supervisor, Copy Staff

Copyright

Contents

Chapter 1

Food, Wonderful Food — How to Cook Your Best

In the distant future, computerized robots may vacuum the house, wash the dishes and even provide you with delicious, home-cooked meals. But for the present, home robots remain largely in the realm of science fiction. Yet, even now there is time-saving equipment available to the home chef — efficient equipment from West Bend that makes food preparation a pleasure instead of a chore. With the equipment that's right for the job and the appealing recipes you'll find in this book, you're sure to enjoy cooking more than ever before.

The Food Preparation System is actually five appliances in one. For example, when you make cakes and cookies such as Bon Bon Pineapple Cake, page 113, or Double Chocolates, page 115, you'll appreciate the efficiency with which it mixes batters. It can whip cream for cappucino and egg whites for Light 'n' Lovely Lemon Pie, page 123. It will knead dough for mouthwatering breads found in Chapter 5, shred cabbage for Apple Cole Slaw, page 97 and grate cheese for tasty treats such as Pecan Cheese Log, page 28. It will grind meats and nuts, and blend beverages, sauces or dressings. In short, it's a compact, easy-to-clean workhorse that will save you hours of lengthy preparations.

For busy people a Slow Cooker is indispensable, because it does the cooking while the cook's away. It's wonderful to come home from a day's work to find Beef Burgundy, page 33 or Lamb and Potato Stew, page 30 ready and waiting and sending forth welcoming aromas. Choose the 4 or 6-quart size, according to your needs. They have various special features, including non-stick interiors. All of them have removable pots that double as rangetop or oven utensils, and are completely immersible for easy cleaning.

For predictable temperatures while frying, simmering, roasting, stewing and baking, you can count on an electric skillet. These all-round meal makers also double as servers. The Sensa-Temp® heat control is removable, so the skillet can be immersed and is dishwasher-safe. The non-stick surfaces are easy to clean. Available in many sizes, these skillets put the fun back into entertaining by making it easy to prepare crowd-size meals. For your next party, try Braised Cornish Game Hens Madeira, page 75, Sole with Fresh Tomato Sauce, page 80, or Stuffed Turkey Breast, page 77, to name just a few of the savory skillet dishes in this book.

A griddle, or pan without sides to get in your way as you maneuver your spatula, is perfect for short-order foods such as pancakes, eggs, and sausages. Besides, this electric griddle is easy to use in a variety of times and places. . . on the kitchen counter for impatient noontime appetites, in the family room to keep snacks warm, as well as at the table for made-to-order break-

fasts. The Sensa-Temp® heat control is detachable for easy cleanup.

Beauty and versatility are the hallmarks of the electric wok with its sloping sides and colorful exterior. Bring it to the table and cook stir-fried vegetables, meats and fish, as guests watch your performance. You can turn inexpensive meat, fish and vegetables into delicious Oriental dishes quickly and easily. Or, it can be used every day for anything from deep-frying onion rings to steaming vegetables. The removable Sensa-Temp® heat control and the non-stick-on aluminum construction makes clean-up extra-easy.

Popcorn — it's everybody's favorite snack, so choose the corn popper to fit your needs. For dieters, there's the Poppery II™ Hot Air Corn Popper that pops 4 quarts of popcorn without oil. Or, for people who think popcorn isn't popcorn unless it's popped with oil, there's the pictured 6-Quart Stir Crazy® Popper. It can't be beat for leaving the fewest unpopped kernels. (The secret is an automatic stirring rod.) Other 4-, 5-and 6-quart size poppers are available.

But popping the corn is just the beginning. Your popped corn can be used in many ways. Look in Chapter 11 for ideas such as Popcorn Honey Cake, Tex Mex, Old-fashioned Molasses Popcorn Balls, and other tempting recipes.

Every office, dorm room, traveler and home should have one. The Hot Pot™ Heat 'n Server with adjustable heat control is perfect for heating water for instants, warming sauces, cooking soups and a variety of other foods and beverages.

Whether it's the first drink in the morning or the final touch to a magnificent meal, coffee has international appeal. In Chapter 11, "Sips and Snacks," you'll find recipes for Viennese, Irish, California and other coffees.

To brew your coffee quickly and keep it good and hot automatically, there's a coffeemaker for the method you prefer – ranging from 3-cup size Percolators to 12-cup Drip Coffeemakers, to 30-cup Party Perks.

Nothing is better for baking than even-heating aluminum baking pieces, coated with an easy-to-clean non-stick surface. There are cookie sheets, loaf pans, cookie and bake pans, pie pans, round and square cake pans, muffin pans, bake and roast pans, and angel food cake pans. These will serve you well for the breads and rolls in Chapter 5, and all the wonderful cakes and cookies in Chapter 9.

Remember, when you place your pans in the oven that the heat must be allowed to circulate evenly around them. If you are using a few pans, arrange them so those pans on lower shelves do not block or absorb heat from those on upper shelves, and so that each pan has at least an inch of space on all sides. Do not use two baking sheets one above the other.

When it comes to cookware, good equipment makes good cooking. Whether it's aluminum or stainless steel, porcelain-coated or polished, you can be sure West Bend craftsmen have constructed it for durability and cooking efficiency.

When you hear the whistle, it's tea time! For a change, try Apple and Pineapple flavored teas (page 135). The Trig® Tea Kettles, in stainless steel or aluminum, are known for their quality-construction, and give years of reliable use.

By the way, it's a good idea to "sweeten" the kettle every few months by boiling in it 2 cups water mixed with 2 cups white vinegar.

Perform a multitude of cooking tasks on your stovetop, with only one utensil — the carbon-steel Wok. It's ideal for stir-frying, steaming, deep-frying, simmering, braising, stewing and serving. With it is included a reversible heating ring for use on gas or electric ranges and an aluminum steamer rack. There are some scrumptious recipes in this book you can make in your wok. Suppose you want to prepare an oriental supper for some friends. You could serve the Chicken Bites, page 20, as an appetizer and Sukiyaki, page 64, as an entreé. Easy and exotic. Serve with a pot of hot tea.

Of course, the complete kitchen needs mixing bowls. These stainless steel mixing bowls come in three different sizes — ¾-quart, 1½-quart and 3-quart. They have flat bases so they will not tip and are shallow enough to accomodate whisks. They are not only easy to clean; they are light and unbreakable and may be heated or chilled.

The handiest bowl in the kitchen, however, is the 3-Quart Grip 'n Whip™ Mixing Bowl with its sturdy handle and convenient pouring lip.

Here's a double-duty bakeware piece; It not only does a superb job at baking cakes, it's also good for roasting and broiling meat, poultry and fish. An added plus – the chrome-plated broiling rack doubles as a cooking rack. And, cleanup is simplified with a non-stick surface.

A kitchen timer frees you from close clock-watching while you're cooking. The Triple Timer™ is an extremely accurate electronic timer that allows you to time three separate activities at once.

With the proper kitchen tools to help you cook your best, and recipes to serve as a guide, you can be adventurous and discover wonderful ways with food, wonderful food!

Chapter 2

The Well-nourished Family — How to Eat Sensibly

More and more families are interested in getting the most nutrition for their food dollars. But there are questions that have been raised about the heathfulness of some eating practices, and since the leading authorities don't agree, it's hard to find answers. In fact, all the answers aren't in yet.

We know we need to eat a wide range of nutrients to maintain good health. We know there is a relationship between obesity and eating more calories than we need and between hypertension and eating a lot of salt. Many experts believe there is a relationship between diet and some forms of cancer and heart diseases. Some studies conclude that we should make dietary changes, but there is still controversy about that.

In the meantime, unless otherwise advised by your doctor, we suggest you follow this plan for nutritional eating developed and long recommended by government nutritionists.

Daily Food Guide

This guide divides foods we need into four basic groups according to their similarity in nutritive value. By following these guidelines you'll be able to choose foods for their vitamins, minerals and proteins as well as their calorie content. The suggested number of servings will average around 1200 calories, depending on the choices made. It provides adequate protein, and will supply most of the vitamins and minerals you need daily. You have to choose foods to meet your special needs. But, remember, you're usually better off eating a wide assortment from these first four groups. The supplemental foods supply mainly calories and little in the way of nutrients.

Bread/Cereal Group

This category consists of all breads and cereals that are whole grain, enriched or restored such as: breads, cooked and ready-to-eat cereals, cornmeal, crackers, flour, grits, macaroni, spaghetti, noodles, rice, rolled oats, quick breads and other baked goods.

Try to have four servings every day. A serving is one slice of bread; ½ cup to ¾ cup cooked cereal, cornmeal, grits, pasta, or rice; two graham crackers, six thin crackers, a 4-inch pancake; or a 5-inch waffle.

Vegetable/Fruit Group

This group includes all vegetables and fruits, particularly those rich in Vitamin A and C. Choose four or more servings daily from this group.

Frequently include a good Vitamin A source (apricots, broccoli, cantaloupe, carrots, all greens, sweet potatoes and hard shell squashes) and every day, one serving of a good Vitamin C source (oranges, grapefruit, orange or grapefruit juice, cantaloupe, fresh or frozen strawberries, broccoli, and green pepper).

A typical serving is: one orange, 4 ounces orange juice, 2 tablespoons raisins, half a medium grapefruit or cantaloupe, juice of one lemon, a wedge of lettuce or one medium potato.

Meat/Fish/Eggs/Legume Group

Take two servings from this group daily. Choose from meats, fish, shellfish, poultry, eggs or cheese, and occasionally substitute dry or canned beans (not green or wax), dry peas and lentils, nuts, or peanut butter.

A sample serving is 2 to 3 ounces (boneless) lean, cooked meat, poultry, or fish or one egg; ½ to ¾ cup cooked dry beans, dry peas, soybeans or lentils; 3 ounces tofu; or 2 tablespoons peanut butter.

Supplemental Foods

As we all know, there are other commonly-eaten foods including butter and margarine; mayonnaise and other salad dressings; sugar and candy; salt and spices; jams and jellies; soft drinks and alcoholic beverages. These foods are used as ingredients in prepared foods; are added to other foods at the table; or are "extras."

Milk Group

Everyone should have something from this group every day although recommended daily servings vary by age. Children under nine should have two to three servings. Children 9 to 12 and pregnant women need three servings. Teenagers and nursing mothers require four servings. For adults, two servings is usually sufficient.

Milk may be whole or skimmed; reconstituted non-fat dry milk; buttermilk; or diluted evaporated milk. Substitutes for milk include cottage cheese and cream cheese; cheddar (natural or processed), Swiss and Parmesan cheese, or ice cream. One serving equals an 8-ounce glass of milk, 1 ounce slice of cheese, 1 cup of plain yogurt, or ½ cup cottage cheese or ice cream.

The amounts of these foods to use depends on the number of calories you require, whether you want to lower your sodium, sugar, fat and cholesterol intake, or increase your starch and fiber consumption, as some health research suggests. Concentrate first on the essentials for your daily diet.

All of this may sound like a big order, but keep in mind that eating right contributes to family health and happiness.

Menu Plans

These illustrate how different foods can be added to a 1200 calorie diet for an adult to increase the caloric level to 1800 and 2400 calories.

1200 calories

Breakfast

Orange juice, ½ cup
Bran flakes with raisins, ½ cup
Milk, whole, ½ cup
Whole-wheat toast, 1 slice
Coffee/Tea

Lunch

Sandwich:
Ham, 2 ounces
Cheese, 1 slice (1 oz.)
Lettuce
Tomato, ½ medium
Enriched bread, 2 slices
Apple, 1 medium
Coffee/Tea

Dinner

Beef, roast, 3 ounces
Baked potato, 1 medium
Broccoli, ½ cup
Milk, skim, 1 cup

Snacks

Cucumber slices, 1 small cucumber
Carrot sticks, 3-4 strips 2-½″ to 3″ long)

1800 calories

Breakfast

Orange juice, ¾ cup
Bran flakes with raisins, ½ cup
Milk, whole, ½ cup
Whole-wheat toast, 1 slice
Jelly, 2 tsp.
Coffee/Tea

Lunch

Sandwich:
Ham, 2 ounces
Cheese, 1 slice (1 oz.)
Lettuce
Tomato, ½ medium
Enriched bread, 2 slices
Salad Dressing, 2 tsp.
Apple, 1 medium
Coffee/Tea

Dinner

Beef roast, 4 ounces
Baked potato, 1 medium
Broccoli, ½ cup
Roll, 1
Margarine, 1 tsp.
Milk, lowfat (1%), 1 cup
Angelfood cake (1/16), with strawberries, ½ cup

Snacks

Peach, fresh, 1 medium

2400 calories

Breakfast

Orange juice, 1 cup
Bran flakes with raisins, ½ cup
Milk, whole, ½ cup
Whole-wheat toast, 1 slice
Jelly, 1 tbsp.
Coffee/Tea

Lunch

Sandwich:
Ham, 2 ounces
Cheese, 1 slice (1 oz.)
Lettuce
Tomato, ½ medium
Enriched bread, 2 slices
Salad Dressing, 2 tsp.
Apple, 1 medium
Plain cookies, 4
Coffee/Tea

Dinner

Beef roast, 5 ounces
Baked potato, 1 medium
Broccoli, ½ cup
Roll, 1
Margarine, 2 tsp.
Milk, lowfat (2%), 1 cup
Angelfood cake (1/12), with strawberries, ½ cup and ice milk, ⅓ cup

Snacks

Peach, fresh, 1 medium
Fruit-flavored yogurt, 1 cup
Banana, 1 small

Helpful Hints:

Think of your day's meals as a whole so you don't overeat or, on the other hand, miss an important food group. And consider more than one day at a time. For example, a special occasion that calls for a piece of Brownie Pie, page 122 shouldn't be prohibited, as long as you can make it up the next day with a lighter dessert such as Fresh Fruit Mold, page 127.

Breakfast is important so don't skip it. Usually people wake up hungry after the night's fast, and perform and feel better in the morning if they've had a good breakfast. Even if it's only fruit juice, try to have a morning meal. Or, use the blender attachment of your Food Preparation System to quickly mix up an energy drink of orange juice, milk, and egg. Try Rice Pancakes with Buttered Blueberry Sauce, page 58, for a special breakfast.

For brown baggers a lunch container with a thermal jug is a smart investment. A wide mouth jug can be used for salads, soups, desserts or beverages. Or prepare sandwiches at a sandwich-making session and freeze up to thirty days. Into the lunch box directly from the freezer, they keep other items chilled and are defrosted by noon. The Fruit Wheat Bread in Chapter 5 is especially good for sandwiches.

For a hot lunch at the office, the Hot Pot ™ Heat 'n Server heats up soup, or leftovers quickly and then cleans up easily.

If you eat your lunch at home it is smart to cook "planovers" at dinner. Simply prepare an extra serving of Lamb and Potato Stew, page 30, in your Slow Cooker or Easy Skillet Chicken Breasts, page 72, in your Electric Skillet — there are any number of possibilities. Heat it up for your lunch the next day, and there you have a "planover."

The evening meal of a protein dish from the meat/fish group, potatoes, vegetables, salad and dessert, need not be a dull repetition. Seasonal foods, the use of substitutes for the usual proteins (legumes, cheese) will change meals pleasantly. There are many recipes to be found throughout this cookbook to help you make your meals more interesting.

Storing foods properly is important, too. Always keep fresh meat, fish and poultry refrigerated. Do not buy — even at bargain prices — any fresh foods which will deteriorate over a short period of refrigerated storage. Keep frozen foods at 0 degrees F. and canned goods in a cool place. Use "first-in/first-out" dating by marking frozen packages and cans with dates, then using the oldest date first.

It's a good idea to start with fresh foods every time if they're available and in their prime.

Between meal snacks can be beneficial, if they are chosen from the basic four food groups. Make your own popsicles from orange juice, lemonade or other fruit juices. Always have fresh fruits and vegetables on hand.

Proper cooking is also important in maintaining the nutritional value of foods. Vegetables should be cooked in as little water as possible or better still, steamed. They should be cooked until just tender crisp. By cooking potatoes in the skin, whether boiled or baked, vitamins and minerals are saved. Stir-frying vegetables in a wok is a healthy method of cooking. The skillets with non-stick surfaces allow you to cook meats, eggs and other pan-fried foods with little or no fat. In the large Dutch ovens with tight-fitting lids meats can be braised with small amounts of liquid thus retaining flavor and nutrition.

Nutritional benefits aside, food must be appealing and enjoyable or it won't be eaten at all. The recipes in this book were developed for dining pleasure. There are some very rich cakes and pies as well as light and tasty fruit and vegetable dishes. We believe that moderation is the best guide in eating to maintain health, and that too stringent a regime can lead to failure in the attempt to have a healthful diet. So, form good eating habits — allowing for some personal indulgences — and may you have a happy, healthy, well-nourished family!

Chapter 3

Appetizers

A tidbit with drinks before dinner has become a part of our life-style. With today's handsome cook and serve equipment it is easy to offer a wide variety of appetizers for any party. Make good use of the wok, the electric skillet and the electric griddle.

Plan appetizers depending on the type of party. If people are invited to dinner, keep the appetizers simple so as not to spoil appetites. Try to have a few low calorie items for dieters.

A more elaborate outlay can be served when it is a cocktail party. For those guests who stay late, a casserole ready to tuck into the oven is a good idea.

Clam Cocktail Fritters

Keep these hot in a low oven or on an electric griddle set at "warm." They are always a popular tidbit.

1 cup all-purpose flour
1 teaspoon baking powder
Dash hot pepper sauce
2 eggs
½ cup stale beer
2 cups minced shucked clams*
¼ cup finely cut green onion
Oil or fat for frying

Mix together flour and baking powder. In a food processor or blender of Food Preparation System, process the flour and baking powder with hot pepper sauce, eggs and beer until smooth. Let stand covered 30 minutes.

Mix batter with clams and onion. Heat 1 to 1½-inches of fat or oil to 375° F. in electric skillet and drop clam mixture by tablespoons into hot fat, frying as many as skillet will hold. Fry fritters on one side about 2 minutes and turn and fry 1 minute longer. Drain on paper towels. Repeat, frying remaining mixture. **Makes about 50.**

* 1 can (7 ounces) minced clams, drained, may be substituted.

Chicken Bites

A Chinese-style hors d'oeuvre.

1 whole chicken breast
1 unbeaten egg white
1 tablespoon cornstarch
1 tablespoon dry sherry
1 tablespoon soy sauce
2 tablespoons vegetable oil
1 clove garlic
½ cup quartered water chestnuts

Bone, remove skin and cut chicken into bite-size pieces. Mix with egg white, cornstarch, sherry and soy sauce. Heat oil in wok over moderately high heat for 2 minutes or in electric wok at 375° F. until hot. Cook garlic in oil while it is heating. Remove garlic. Lift chicken from sauce and stir-fry pieces in oil for 2 to 3 minutes. Add water chestnuts and stir-fry 1 or 2 minutes longer. With a slotted spoon put chicken and chestnuts into a dish and serve with toothpicks. **Makes about 25.**

Beer 'n Hot Dog Puffs

Fun for a party.

¼ cup butter
½ cup boiling beer
½ cup all-purpose flour
½ teaspoon salt
2 eggs
3 ground up hot dogs*
1 teaspoon prepared mustard

Combine butter and beer in a small saucepan. Keep over low heat until butter is melted. Add flour and salt all at once and stir over low heat until mixture forms a ball which leaves sides of pan. Remove from heat. Add eggs one at a time, beating well after each addition. Beat in hot dogs and mustard. Batter should hold its shape when lifted from a spoon.

Drop by teaspoons onto a non-stick baking sheet. Bake at 425° F. about 20 minutes. The puffs can be made in advance, frozen and crisped in a hot oven for a few minutes at serving time. Even if made in advance and not frozen, you may want to crisp them at serving time. **Makes about 4 dozen.**

Note: The grinder of the Food Preparation System can be used for grinding the hot dogs, and the mixer with the stirrer for addition of the eggs and other ingredients. Beat on speed No. 4 until batter holds its shape when lifted with a spoon.

* If hot dogs have a thick skin, remove before grinding.

Cheese and Sausage Tidbits

A tangy appetizer.

½ pound grated sharp cheese
¼ pound hot Italian sausage
¼ pound breakfast sausage
1½ cups buttermilk biscuit mix
½ cup chopped salted peanuts
Catsup

Mix all ingredients except catsup together until well blended. (If bulk sausage is not available, remove skins from links.) Shape into 1-inch balls. Place on a non-stick 15½ x 10½ x 1-inch pan and bake at 350° F. for 30 minutes. Serve warm with catsup for a dip. **Makes about 50.**

Stuffed Mushrooms

Prepare the mushrooms in advance and tuck into the oven in time to serve hot.

16 medium sized mushrooms
¼ cup minced green onion
4 tablespoons butter
½ cup minced cooked chicken
½ cup fine dry, bread crumbs
½ teaspoon dried rosemary leaves
2 tablespoons chopped parsley
Salt and freshly ground pepper to taste
Melted butter

Remove stems from mushroom caps, trim and chop finely. Set caps aside. Sauté stems and green onion in a skillet in 2 tablespoons butter until tender. Combine with remaining ingredients including the 2 tablespoons butter. Season to taste. Wipe mushrooms with dampened paper towel and brush with melted butter. Put them hollow side up in a buttered baking dish and fill with chicken mixture. Bake at 375° F. for 20 to 25 minutes or until lightly browned. **Makes 16.**

Vegetable Dip

Cuts off a few party calories.

½ cup mayonnaise
1 cup plain low fat yogurt
½ cup dairy sour cream
1 envelope Bloody Mary cocktail mix
⅛ teaspoon salt
2 green onions, sliced, both green and white
Chopped fresh parsley
Celery and carrot sticks
Thinly sliced raw turnips

Mix mayonnaise, yogurt, sour cream, cocktail mix and salt until well blended. Stir in green onions. Chill overnight. Serve in bowl garnished with parsley and surrounded by vegetables for dipping. **Makes 1½ or 2 cups.**

Shrimp Fritters

Surely the first food to disappear at every gathering.

½ pound small shrimp
2 green onions
1 carrot
1 cup water
¾ cup all-purpose flour
2 small or 1 large egg
1 teaspoon salt
¾ teaspoon curry powder
⅛ teaspoon ground cumin
1 garlic clove
Freshly ground pepper to taste
Fat or oil for frying

Peel, devein and split shrimp lengthwise. Cut green onions into 1-inch pieces, including 3 inches of green tops. Peel and cut carrots into 1-inch julienne strips.

Combine water, flour, eggs, salt, curry powder, cumin and garlic clove which has been put through a press. Mix with a whisk until well blended. Add shrimp, vegetables, season to taste with pepper and mix well.

In the electric skillet heat fat or oil to 375° F., having it at least 1-inch deep. Fill a tablespoon with batter and pour carefully into hot fat. Fry about 2 minutes on one side and turn and fry 1 minute longer. Fry as many as the skillet will hold at one time. Drain on paper towels and keep hot. Repeat, frying remaining batter. (The little fritters can be kept hot in a 250° F. oven or on electric griddle set at "warm.") **Makes about 2½ dozen small fritters.**

Fruit Spread

Serve this with toasted whole wheat crackers as a pleasant change.

1 cup chunky peanut butter
¼ cup honey
¼ cup wheat germ
¼ cup apricot preserves

Mix all ingredients lightly together. Serve at room temperature with crisp whole wheat crackers. **Makes about 1½ cups.**

Garlic Mushrooms

Serve with picks for an appetizer, or add to a salad for an unusual flavor.

1 pound fresh button mushrooms
3 tablespoons peanut or vegetable oil
½ cup dry white wine
½ cup water
2 tablespoons wine vinegar
½ teaspoon salt
¼ teaspoon dill seed
¼ teaspoon ground cumin
Freshly ground pepper to taste
2 cloves garlic
3 tablespoons chopped fresh parsley

Trim and wipe mushrooms with a damp cloth. Combine with oil, wine, water, vinegar, seasonings, garlic and parsley in a saucepan. Cover and simmer 30 minutes. Put mushrooms and liquid into a glass container which can be covered and store in refrigerator for several days or several weeks. Remove from liquid to serve. **Makes about 1 quart.**

Stuffed Eggs

Hard-cooked egg halves are adaptable. You can vary the fillings to suit the menu.

12 hard-cooked eggs
1 cup cooked crab meat, flaked
1 cup finely chopped celery
2 tablespoons finely chopped green pepper
1 tablespoon French salad dressing mix
⅓ cup dairy sour cream

Slice eggs in half lengthwise. Remove yolks and mash. Combine yolks, crab meat, celery, green pepper, salad dressing mix and sour cream, blending well. Stir until well mixed. Refill egg whites. Chill, covered with plastic wrap or wax paper until serving time. **Makes 24 stuffed eggs.**

Variations:
Omit crab meat and add 6 slices of crumbled, cooked bacon to the basic yolk mixture.

Omit crab meat and add 2 cans (3 ounces each) deviled ham to the basic yolk mixture.

Swedish Liver Paté

Delicious for a first course or on the buffet table.

1 pound calves liver
¼ pound boneless veal
½ pound fresh pork fat
1 large onion
8 anchovy fillets
4 tablespoons all-purpose flour
3 eggs
1⅓ cups cream
2 teaspoons salt
½ teaspoon white pepper
⅔ pound pork fat cut in thin slices

Cut liver, veal and pork fat into cubes and grind or process together with onion and anchovies until very smooth. Beat together flour, eggs, cream, salt and pepper and add gradually to liver mixture, beating until well blended.

Line an oblong mold or a non-stick 9 x 5 x 3-inch loaf pan with thin slices of pork fat. Fill ¾ full with mixture and cover tightly with aluminum foil. Place in a hot water bath and bake at 250° F. for 1½ hours. Keep in mold and chill overnight in refrigerator. Unmold and serve in thin slices with rye bread and pickles. Will keep 7 to 10 days when refrigerated. **Makes 10 - 12 servings.**

Note: The grinder of the Food Preparation System may be used to grind the meats and the bowl and stirrer for mixing.

Hot Cheese Wafers

Crisp morsels to serve with the first course or at the witching hour.

1 pound sharp cheddar cheese, grated
½ cup butter or margarine
1 cup all-purpose flour
Paprika

Mix cheese, butter, and flour until well blended. Shape into 2 rolls 2-inches in diameter and roll in paprika. Wrap in plastic wrap and chill overnight in refrigerator. Slice very thin and bake at 425° F. for about 6 minutes. **Makes about 36 wafers.**

Note: Use the Food Preparation System to prepare this recipe. The cheese can be grated using fine grater blade No. 5 with slicer/shredder accessory, and the mixture mixed in the mixing bowl with the stirrer on Speed No. 3.

Cossack Shrimp

A saucy shrimp with a vodka fillip.

2 pounds medium-size raw shrimp
¼ cup peanut oil
2 tablespoons Worcestershire sauce
¼ cup vodka
¼ cup tomato juice
1 clove garlic, finely minced
Dash hot pepper sauce
Lemon slices

Peel and devein shrimp. Heat oil in wok over moderately high heat for 2 minutes or in electric wok at 375° F. Add shrimp and stir-fry for 2 minutes or until shrimp just turns pink. Add remaining ingredients except lemon slices and stir until hot. Remove from heat, add lemon slices, cool and chill in refrigerator. Serve in bowl with picks. **Makes about 40 shrimp.**

Spicy Tomato Dip

This can be prepared in advance and stored in the refrigerator for several days.

¼ cup instant minced onion
¼ teaspoon instant minced garlic
¼ cup water
1 tablespoon olive oil
1 can (1 pound) tomatoes, broken up
1½ tablespoons Worcestershire sauce
1 teaspoon chili powder
Dash sugar
Salt and freshly ground pepper to taste

Combine onion, garlic and water and let stand 10 to 15 minutes to rehydrate. Drain. Sauté in oil in a small saucepan. Add remaining ingredients and simmer, uncovered, 15 minutes. Chill. Spoon into a serving dish and surround with corn chips, shrimp, potato chips, avocado cubes or other vegetables of your choice to use as dippers. **Makes about 1¼ cups.**

Cheese and Tuna Dip

Easy to prepare. Chill until ready to serve.

1 package (8 ounces) cream cheese, softened
4 tablespoons mayonnaise
1 tablespoon lemon juice
1 teaspoon prepared mustard
1 can (7 or 7½ ounces) tuna fish, drained
1 small green pepper, seeded and finely chopped

Mix all ingredients until blended. Serve with crackers, chips or crisp vegetables. **Makes 1½ cups.**

Cheese, Tomato, and Beef Spread

A savory spread that will keep for several weeks in the refrigerator.

½ pound cheddar cheese
½ cup fresh tomatoes, seeded, peeled and chopped
¼ cup butter or margarine
¼ pound dried beef, finely chopped
1 teaspoon onion juice
Assorted crackers

Melt cheese over low heat in 2-quart saucepan. Add tomatoes gradually, stirring constantly. Blend in butter, dried beef and onion juice. Store in refrigerator, but let stand at room temperature about an hour before serving. Serve in a pretty crock surrounded with crackers. Provide a knife for spreading. **Makes about 1½ cups.**

Pecan Cheese Log

An unusual Georgia pecan creation which will get raves.

1 cup whole canned tomatoes, drained
1 package (8 ounces) cream cheese, softened
2 cups (8 ounces) grated cheddar cheese
½ cup butter or margarine, softened
½ cup chopped onion
½ teaspoon salt
1 cup chopped pecans

Combine tomatoes, cream cheese, cheddar cheese, butter, onion and salt in bowl and beat until smooth. Spoon out onto 2 pieces of wax paper and roll with paper to form two logs. Place in freezer 1 hour or until firm. Remove wax paper and smooth rolls. Cover with chopped pecans. Keep chilled until serving time. Serve with crackers, chips, Melba toast.**Makes 2 rolls.**

Note: Use bowl of Food Preparation System with stirrer. Start at speed No. 2 until partially blended and then speed No. 3 or No. 4 until smooth.

Peanut Butter Canapes

These rolled canapes can be made in advance and chilled until time to toast. Cover with lightly dampened paper towels during storage.

1 cup chunky peanut butter
½ cup chili sauce
1 egg
2 tablespoons grated horseradish
15 slices thin sliced bread
¼ cup melted butter

Mix peanut butter, chili sauce, egg and horseradish until well blended.

Trim crusts from bread. Place one heaping tablespoon of peanut butter mixture on each slice; spread evenly over surfaces. Roll as for jelly roll and secure with toothpicks. Brush with melted butter. Place on broiler pan and toast 3-inches from source of heat until toasty brown, about 3 minutes. Cut in half crosswise to serve. If desired, keep warm for serving on electric griddle set at "warm" setting. **Makes 30.**

Chapter 4

Soups and Stews

Soups and stews are the backbone of many of our menus. With a slow cooker, electric skillet or a good range top skillet or saucepan, they can be prepared with ease.

Recipes for soups and stews can be the base for your own imagination to take over. Have a little fun adding a bit of this or that.

Make up your own bouquet garni combination and add it to a recipe for a change of flavor. Experimenting is half the fun of cooking.

Herbed Chicken Stew

Put on to cook in late morning; a treat will be ready at dinner time. Serve greens laced with orange sections and lots of hot French bread with it.

1 broiler-fryer, about 3½ pounds
2 tablespoons butter
½ cup diced ham
½ teaspoon salt
¼ teaspoon leaf thyme
¼ teaspoon marjoram
½ teaspoon tarragon
1 clove garlic, minced
2 carrots, peeled and diced
2 onions, diced
½ cup dry white wine
½ cup chicken bouillon
2 potatoes, peeled and diced

Cut chicken into serving pieces, saving bony pieces for some other use. Brown pieces in slow cooker pot in butter over medium heat of range unit. Transfer cooking pot to heating base using hot pads and add remaining ingredients. Cover and slow cook at setting No. 3 for 6 to 8 hours. **Makes 4 servings.**

Lamb and Potato Stew

A simple but delicious combination.

½ cup butter or margarine, melted
1 large onion, chopped
1 teaspoon salt
Freshly ground pepper to taste
2 teaspoons dried rosemary leaves
1½ pounds boneless lamb cubes
3 cups peeled potatoes, cut in 1-inch cubes
2 large tomatoes

Pour butter into an 8 cup (2-quart) casserole which can be tightly covered. Add onion, salt, pepper, crushed rosemary leaves, lamb cubes and potatoes. Stir to mix ingredients. Cut tomatoes in half crosswise and place cut side down on lamb mixture in casserole. Cover and bake at 400° F. for 1¼ to 1½ hours. **Makes 4 servings.**

Note: This stew can also be cooked in the slow cooker. Assemble ingredients as directed in the cooker pot; cover and cook at setting No. 3 for 5 to 6 hours.

Veal Empire

Veal Empire is a dish fit for a king. Serve with new red potatoes in the skin and steamed zucchini squash.

2 pounds veal for stew
3 tablespoons all-purpose flour
½ teaspoon salt
Freshly ground pepper to taste
½ teaspoon dried tarragon leaves
4 tablespoons butter or margarine
1 clove garlic, finely chopped
1 carrot, finely chopped
1 teaspoon grated lemon rind
1 cup mushrooms, sliced
1 cup dry white wine
1 cube chicken bouillon
½ cup water

Dredge veal with flour that has been mixed with salt, pepper and crushed tarragon leaves. Heat butter in the electric skillet at 350° F. and brown meat, garlic and carrot. If any flour mixture does not cling to meat, add now. Then add remaining ingredients and reduce heat to "simmer" setting. Cover with vent closed and simmer for 45 minutes or until veal is fork tender. Remove lid and allow liquid to reduce to a small amount. Serve with veal. **Makes 4 to 6 servings.**

Pork Stew with Dumplings

A good cold weather meal.

1½ pounds cubed raw pork
¼ cup all-purpose flour
3 tablespoons butter or margarine
1 clove garlic, diced
1 teaspoon salt
Freshly ground pepper to taste
3 cups boiling water
2 chicken bouillon cubes
2 tablespoons celery tops, chopped
1 teaspoon dried sage
12 small whole onions
4 medium carrots, peeled, cut in 2-inch pieces

Mix pork and flour and brown in butter in slow cooker pot over medium heat. Transfer to heating base, using hot pads. Add remaining ingredients. Cover and cook at setting No. 3 for 8 hours. Raise to setting No. 5, drop dumplings on top and cook covered for 30 minutes more.

Dumplings: Mix together 1½ cups all-purpose flour, 2 teaspoons baking powder and ½ teaspoon salt. Cut in 1 tablespoon shortening. Fold in ¾ cup milk only until blended. Drop by tablespoons on stew in slow cooker and cook covered 30 minutes. **Makes 4 to 6 servings.**

Beef Burgundy

A flavorful stew laced with wine and brandy.

¼ cup all-purpose flour
½ teaspoon salt
Freshly ground pepper to taste
2 pounds cubed beef
1 tablespoon vegetable oil
1 tablespoon butter
2 large carrots, peeled, diced
2 medium leeks, cleaned, diced
2 medium onions, diced
2 garlic cloves, pressed
2 tablespoons chopped fresh parsley
2 tablespoons snipped fresh chives
1½ cups burgundy wine
2 tablespoons brandy
1 bouquet garni of ¼ teaspoon thyme, 1 bay leaf, ¼ teaspoon rosemary

Mix together flour, salt and pepper and roll beef cubes in mixture. Heat oil and butter in slow cooker pot on medium heat of range unit. Add beef and brown, stirring. Transfer pot to heating base, using hot pads.

Add remaining ingredients. Cover and slow cook at setting No. 4 for 5 hours. Reduce to setting No. 2 for serving. Remove bouquet garni and serve with hot cooked noodles. **Makes 4 to 6 servings.**

Chicken Soup

This time-honored soup hits the spot on a cool day.

¼ cup chicken fat
1 large onion, finely minced
1 carrot, finely minced
1 stalk celery, finely minced
3 tablespoons all-purpose flour
3½ cups chicken broth
1 cup finely chopped cooked chicken
¼ cup chopped fresh parsley

Heat chicken fat in a saucepan and sauté onion, carrot and celery on low heat for about 10 minutes, stirring. Mix in flour and cook 2 minutes. Add chicken broth, chicken and parsley and bring to a boil. Serve at once. **Makes 4½ cups.**

Turkey Soup

You can use the bones from Stuffed Turkey Breast (page 77) for this recipe.

Bones from turkey
About 2 quarts cold water
½ cup chopped onion
½ cup chopped celery
½ cup chopped carrots
Several sprigs parsley
Salt and freshly ground pepper to taste

Break up turkey bones. Place in a large saucepan or Dutch Oven with water to cover. Add vegetables. Cover and simmer gently 2 to 3 hours, skimming if necessary. Strain and season to taste with salt and pepper. Serve clear or add some leftover meat, boiled rice, finely diced cooked vegetables or Cracker Crumb Dumplings. **Makes about 6 servings.**

Cracker Crumb Dumplings

1 egg, slightly beaten
⅛ teaspoon salt
Freshly ground pepper to taste
Garlic, onion, or celery salt to taste
Cracker crumbs

To slightly beaten egg, add seasonings and enough cracker crumbs to make a mixture which will hold its shape. Make into tiny balls. Drop into rapidly boiling soup, and poach about 10 minutes, uncovered. **Makes about 20-24 dumplings, or enough for 6 servings of soup.**

Fish Soup

A hearty lunch soup gives you energy for an active afternoon.

1 medium potato, peeled and diced
1 cup stewed tomatoes
1 small onion, diced
1 stalk celery, diced
½ teaspoon salt
Freshly ground pepper to taste
2 cups boiling water
¼ cup chopped fresh parsley
1 cup diced boneless raw white fish, about ½ pound

Combine vegetables, salt, pepper and boiling water in a 2-quart saucepan.
Cover and simmer 15 to 20 minutes until potatoes are tender. Add parsley
and fish and cook below the boiling point about 5 minutes. **Makes about
4½ cups.**

Arizona Chili

If you prefer a thicker chili, use less water. Serve with crackers, or, as many Arizonians do, crisp lettuce leaves.

1 pound coarsely ground beef
1 can (1 pound) kidney or red beans and liquid
1 can (6 ounces) tomato paste
2 cups chopped onion
3 tablespoons chili powder
1 tablespoon ground cumin
Salt to taste
2 cups water

Brown beef in a 3¾-quart saucepan. Pour off excess fat. Stir in beans and
liquid, tomato paste, onions and seasonings. Add water to give desired
consistency. Bring to a boil and cook slowly over low heat, covered, until
onions are tender, about one hour. Stir occasionally. **Makes 4 to 6
servings.**

Beef Barley Soup

A rich soup which ideally takes two days to make.

To make stock:

2 pounds beef neck bones
1 onion
1 stalk celery
8 peppercorns
½ teaspoon salt
1½ quarts water

Ask at the meat counter for beef neck bones as they are particulary good for beef barley soup. If not available, buy beef soup bones but get 3 or 4 pounds.

Combine bones with remaining ingredients in a large saucepan or Dutch Oven and bring to a boil. Skim froth, if necessary. Reduce heat and simmer 3 to 4 hours. Cool enough to handle. Strain stock and refrigerate overnight. Remove fat. There should be 4 to 5 cups. Cool meat bones. Remove meat and dice. Refrigerate.

To make soup:

4 to 5 cups beef stock
¼ cup barley
1 leek
1 cup canned tomatoes
1 carrot, peeled and diced
Meat from bones
Salt to taste
Chopped fresh parsley

Combine beef stock and barley and cook, covered, 30 minutes. Clean leek well and dice, using only the white part. Add with tomatoes, carrot, meat and salt to taste to broth and simmer 30 minutes longer. Serve topped with fresh chopped parsley. **Makes about 6 (1 cup) servings.**

Split Pea Soup with Meatballs

This soup is perfect to serve after a football game or other winter activity. Lots of rye bread and butter and an assortment of fresh fruit will please hungry fans.

5 cups chicken stock
½ pound split peas (about 1 cup)
1 large onion, chopped
½ teaspoon crushed dried rosemary leaves
½ pound ground beef
¼ pound sausage
1 tablespoon Worcestershire sauce
1 clove garlic, minced
¼ cup dry bread crumbs
1 egg

Bring chicken stock to a boil in large saucepan or Dutch Oven and add peas, onion and rosemary and simmer covered, about 1 hour. Stir occasionally.

Mix ground beef, sausage, Worcestershire sauce, garlic, bread crumbs and egg until well blended. Make tiny meat balls. Drop into boiling soup and simmer 30 minutes longer. **Makes about 8 cups.**

Elegant Mushroom Soup

Serve this quickly-made soup as a luncheon soup for two or a first course for four.

1 slice bacon
½ leek
¼ teaspoon crushed dried rosemary
1 can (10¾ ounces) cream of mushroom soup
1 soup can water
1 envelope instant chicken bouillon

Dice bacon and fry in a small saucepan until crisp. Remove bacon from pan and reserve. Clean and chop leek and sauté in bacon fat until tender, but not browned. Add rosemary and mushroom soup. Stir in water gradually and add bouillon. Bring to a boil and serve topped with crisp bacon. **Makes about 3 cups.**

Leek and Potato Soup

Bacon adds heartiness to this soup. Serve in large bowls for lunch with toasted peanut butter sandwiches.

4 or 5 slices bacon
1 large leek
1 large potato
1 tablespoon rice
1 cup water
2½ cups milk
Salt and freshly ground pepper to taste

Cut bacon crosswise and sauté in a saucepan until cooked. Cut leek in half lengthwise and separate leaves to wash out sand. Cut both green and white parts crosswise into ½-inch slices. Sauté with bacon until leek is wilted, 3 to 4 minutes. Peel potato and dice. Add to leek with rice and water. Bring to a boil, cover and simmer 15 to 20 minutes until potatoes are tender. Add milk and heat to boiling point. Season to taste with salt and pepper. **Makes about 6 cups.**

Asparagus Soup

A delightful spring soup to serve as a first course.

1 medium onion, chopped
1 medium potato, peeled and diced
1½ cups peeled, sliced asparagus ends
2 chicken bouillon cubes
Water to cover
2 tablespoons all-purpose flour
2 cups milk
⅛ teaspoon nutmeg
1 stalk asparagus, cut in very thin slices

Combine onion, potato, asparagus ends, bouillon cubes and water to cover in a medium saucepan. Cook until tender, about 15 minutes. Puree with flour in food processor or blender of Food Preparation System until smooth. Return to saucepan. Stir in milk and nutmeg with whisk and heat to boiling point. To serve, garnish with thin slices of asparagus. **Makes about 5 cups.**

Corn Chowder

Hearty luncheon or supper soup. Add a sandwich and fruit to make the meal.

¼ cup chopped green pepper
¼ cup chopped onion
¼ cup butter or margarine
3 medium potatoes, peeled and diced
Freshly ground pepper to taste
1 teaspoon salt
2 cups water
1 can (17 ounces) cream style corn
2 cups whole milk
1 cup evaporated milk
Chopped fresh parsley

In a 3 quart saucepan sauté pepper and onion in butter until tender over medium heat. Add potatoes, pepper, salt and water. Bring to a boil, cover and simmer until potatoes are tender, about 15 minutes. Add remaining ingredients and heat, stirring, until chowder bubbles. **Makes about 10 servings.**

Quick Cheese Soup

Here's how to enhance canned cheese soup.

1 can (about 10½ ounces) condensed cheddar cheese soup
1 medium onion, finely chopped
½ cup finely diced celery
1 can (11 ounces) condensed beef broth
1 soup can water
Popped corn

Combine all ingredients, except popcorn, in a 2- quart saucepan, stirring to blend well. Simmer, covered, for 5 to 10 minutes, stirring occasionally. Serve topped with popcorn. **Makes about 4 servings.**

Navy Bean Soup

A filling soup, made easy by the slow cooker.

1 pound navy beans
2½ quarts water
1 small carrot, diced
1 medium onion, chopped
1 medium potato, peeled and diced
1½ teaspoons salt
1 ham bone or shank

Wash and sort navy beans. Soak in water overnight in slow cooker pot. When ready to cook, add remaining ingredients and cook 6 hours on setting No. 3. Remove ham bone and cut off meat. Dice and return to soup. Season to taste with additional salt and pepper, if desired. **Makes 6 to 8 servings.**

If desired, the process may be reversed. Soak the beans during the day and cook the soup overnight.

Chapter 5

Breads, Rolls and Pancakes

If you haven't yet, you must try baking your own breads and rolls. It is a way to get variety into your meals, and can transform a simple meal into a superb one just by adding an elegant bread. Non-stick bakeware is a boon to the "baker" in both the baking and clean-up. If you own a Food Preparation System, the mixer bowl with dough hook does the kneading for you. When baking breads, rolls, muffins, cakes, etc., always pre-heat the oven and grease pans well, if non-stick pans are not available.

Brioche

These rich yeast rolls will make any meal a feast.

¼ cup milk
1 cup butter
⅓ cup sugar
1 teaspoon salt
2 packages active dry yeast
¼ cup lukewarm water, 110° F.
4 eggs
4½ cups all-purpose flour
1 egg white

Combine milk, butter, sugar and salt in a saucepan over low heat until butter is almost melted. In a large bowl soften yeast in water. When butter is cooled, add to yeast with eggs and beat well for 2 minutes. Add 3 cups flour and beat for 4 minutes. Add remaining flour and beat until batter is smooth. Cover and let rise in a warm place until doubled in bulk. Stir down. Cover tightly with aluminum foil and chill overnight in the refrigerator.

Take dough from refrigerator and divide into 2 pieces, ¾ and ¼. Cut larger piece into 24 equal parts and shape into smooth round balls. Place one ball in each muffin cup of a well-greased or non-stick 2½ x 1¼-inch muffin pan. Cut smaller piece of dough into 24 equal parts and make 24 small round balls. Make a deep indentation in each large ball, dampen bottom of small ball with water and press into each indentation. Cover, let rise in a warm place until double in bulk. Beat egg white with a fork and with a brush, carefully spread on each brioche. Bake at 375° F. for 15 minutes or until browned lightly. **Makes 2 dozen.**

Note: If using the mixer of the Food Preparation System, use the dough hook with the bowl and beat on speed No. 2 for the first beating and speed No. 4 for the second.

White Bread

This recipe makes 4 loaves but since bread freezes well it is a bonus. It's a light-textured bread.

2 packages active dry yeast
1 cup lukewarm water, 110° F.
5 tablespoons sugar
2 tablespoons salt
4 cups lukewarm milk
12 cups (about) all-purpose flour
5 tablespoons shortening

In a large bowl combine yeast, water and 1 teaspoon of the sugar and let stand until bubbly, about 10 minutes. Add remaining sugar, salt and milk and start adding flour mixing well with a spoon. When almost all of the flour is in, add shortening and blend into flour mixture. Add additional flour as needed to make dough stiff enough to knead. Turn dough out on a floured board and knead until dough is smooth and elastic, about 10 minutes. Place in a greased bowl and turn to grease dough. Cover with plastic wrap and a towel and let rise in a warm place until double in bulk (about 2 hours). Punch down and let rise again until double in bulk (about 1 hour). Divide dough into 4 portions. Shape into loaves and put into 9 x 5 x 3-inch non-stick loaf pans. Grease tops. Cover and let rise in a warm place until doubled. Bake at 375° F. for 45 to 50 minutes. Remove from pans and cool on rack. For a soft crust, butter tops of loaves while warm. **Makes 4 loaves.**

Note: To use the Food Preparation System, combine yeast, water, sugar and milk as directed using dough hook on speed No. 2. Add flour gradually and beat for 4 to 5 minutes on speed No. 4. Add shortening as directed toward end of flour addition.

French Bread

Two crusty loaves, of which you will be very proud.

2 cups hot water
2 teaspoons salt
1 tablespoon sugar
2 tablespoons shortening
2 packages active dry yeast
8 cups (about) all-purpose flour
¼ cup yellow corn meal
½ teaspoon salt
½ cup cold water
1½ teaspoons cornstarch

Combine hot water, 2 teaspoons salt, sugar and shortening in a bowl. When cooled to lukewarm mix in yeast to dissolve. Add half of the flour and beat until smooth. Add remaining flour until dough is stiff enough to knead. Knead until smooth and elastic. Place in a greased bowl, turn to grease dough, cover with plastic wrap and a towel and let rise in a warm place until double in bulk (about 2 hours). Punch down. Divide into two pieces on a slightly-floured board and shape into two long narrow loaves. Place on a 17 x 14-inch non-stick baking sheet sprinkled with corn meal. While bread is rising the first time, combine ½ teaspoon salt with cold water and cornstarch and cook until clear. Cool.

Brush on loaves several times during rising. Let loaves rise until very light. When ready to bake, cut diagonal slices on top of loaves about 2-inches apart using scissors. Put a bread pan full of boiling water beside or above baking sheet and bake bread at 350° F. about 50 minutes or until bread is browned and crusty. Cool loaves on rack. **Makes 2 loaves.**

Note: If you have a Food Preparation System use dough hook. Mix for 1 minute at speed No. 1 for first half of process. Add remaining flour and mix at speed No. 2 for 3 to 4 minutes.

Fruit Wheat Bread

This fruity bread makes wonderful sandwiches or is just plain good slathered with butter.

⅔ cup chopped dried apricots
½ cup uncooked oatmeal
¼ cup dark brown sugar, firmly packed
2 teaspoons salt
1 tablespoon vegetable oil
2 cups boiling water
2 packages active dry yeast
1 egg, beaten
1 cup chopped raisins
¾ cup almonds, chopped
½ cup wheat germ
1½ cups non-fat dry milk powder
3 cups whole wheat flour
2½ cups all-purpose flour
Melted butter

In a bowl combine apricots, oatmeal, sugar, salt, oil and boiling water. Stir and allow to cool to room temperature. When cooled add yeast, egg, raisins, almonds, wheat germ and dried milk. Mix well. Add whole wheat flour and beat well to combine. Add enough all-purpose flour to make a stiff dough.

Measure 1 cup all-purpose flour onto a smooth surface and turn bread mixture out onto flour. Knead 10 minutes, adding more flour, if necessary.

Put dough into a greased bowl, turn to grease dough. Cover with plastic wrap and a towel and let rise in a warm place until double in bulk.

Punch down. Cut into 2 pieces. Let rest 10 minutes. Shape into loaves and put into non-stick 9 x 5 x 3-inch loaf pans. Cover and let rise again until double in bulk. Bake at 350° F. for 40 minutes or until nicely browned. Remove from pans to rack. Brush with melted butter. **Makes 2 loaves.**

Note: If using the Food Preparation System, the whole process can be done in the mixer bowl using the dough hook. After the oatmeal mixture has cooled proceed with the addition of yeast and flours and mix on speed No. 2 and knead on speed No. 3 or No. 4.

Breakfast Loaves

Slice, toast, butter and serve with marmalade.

2 packages active dry yeast
6 cups all-purpose flour
¼ teaspoon baking soda
1 tablespoon sugar
2 teaspoons salt
¾ cup non-fat dry milk powder
2½ cups hot (120° to 130° F.) water
3 tablespoons corn meal

Combine yeast, 3 cups flour, soda, sugar, salt and dry milk. Add hot water and beat well. Stir in rest of flour to make a stiff batter. (Batter should hold shape when a spoon is lifted from it.) Lightly grease two non-stick 9 x 5 x 3-inch loaf pans and sprinkle with corn meal. Spoon batter into pans and sprinkle top with corn meal. Cover and let rise in a warm place for 45 minutes, or until batter is even with top of pan. Bake at 400° F. for 25 minutes. Remove from pans immediately and cool on rack. **Makes 2 loaves.**

This bread should be frozen if it is not used within a few days.

Note: If using the Food Preparation System, use bowl with stirrer at speeds No. 3 and No. 4.

Oatmeal Wheat Bread

Freezes well for future treats of homemade bread.

4 cups boiling water
3 cups raw quick-cooking oatmeal
½ cup lukewarm water
1 teaspoon sugar
2 packages active dry yeast
2 cups whole wheat flour
2 tablespoons salt
½ cup molasses
4 tablespoons melted shortening
7 cups all-purpose flour

Pour boiling water over oatmeal in a large bowl. Cover and let stand until lukewarm. Mix together the lukewarm water, sugar and yeast and let stand until bubbly. Add to lukewarm oatmeal with whole wheat flour. Beat well and let rise until light and bubbly, about 1 hour.

Add salt, molasses, shortening and about 6 cups of the all-purpose flour and blend well. If necessary, add more flour so that dough is stiff enough to knead. Knead until smooth and elastic. Place in a greased bowl, turn to grease dough, cover with plastic wrap and a towel and let rise in a warm place until double in bulk (about 2 hours). Punch down. Divide and shape into 3 loaves. Place in 9 x 5 x 3-inch non-stick pans. Grease tops. Cover and let rise until double in bulk. Bake at 350° F. for 45 to 50 minutes or until well browned. Remove from pans and cool on rack. **Makes 3 loaves.**

Whole Wheat Bread

A moist loaf that freezes well.

1 teaspoon sugar
1 cup lukewarm water, 110° F.
2 packages active dry yeast
1 cup non-fat dry milk powder
4 cups whole wheat flour
3 tablespoons vegetable oil
3 tablespoons honey
2 cups hot water
4 teaspoons salt
5 cups all-purpose flour

Combine sugar, water and yeast in a bowl and let stand until foamy, about 10 minutes. In another bowl combine non-fat dry milk with 2 cups whole wheat flour, oil, honey and hot water. Beat well. Mix with yeast, and cover and let stand in a warm place for 30 minutes. Add rest of whole wheat flour and salt and beat well. Add white flour to form a dough stiff enough to knead. Turn out on a floured surface and knead until smooth and elastic, about 10 minutes. Place in a greased bowl and turn to grease dough. Cover with plastic wrap and a towel and let rise in a warm place until doubled in bulk. Shape into 3 loaves and place in non-stick 9 x 5 x 3-inch loaf pans. Grease tops. Cover and let rise until double in bulk. Bake at 375° F. for about 35 minutes. Remove from pans and cool on rack. If a soft crust is desired, rub crust with butter. **Makes 3 loaves.**

Note: If the Food Preparation System is being used, set yeast, sugar and water in bowl. Add flour/milk mixture to yeast and beat with stirrer on speed No. 2 until smooth. Cover, let stand 30 minutes. Add remaining flour and salt and beat with dough hook for about 2 minutes on speed No. 2 or until a smooth elastic dough is formed.

One Two Three Rolls

These are easy to make. If 4 dozen is too many to use at one time, these little rolls can be frozen for future use.

¼ cup sugar
½ cup butter, softened
½ teaspoon salt
2 eggs at room temperature
¾ cup scalded milk
2 packages active dry yeast
4 cups all-purpose flour
½ cup melted butter

Beat sugar, softened butter, salt and eggs together in a large bowl. Cool milk and add with yeast to egg mixture. Beat in flour. Cover dough with plastic wrap and a cloth and let rise until double in bulk. Turn out on a floured board and cut into 6 pieces. Roll each piece into a thin round. Cut into 8 pie-shaped pieces. Spread with melted butter and roll from wide side. Shape into a crescent and place on non-stick baking sheet. Continue with remaining dough to make 4 dozen. Spread rolls with melted butter and let rise until double in bulk. Bake at 425° F. for 12 to 15 minutes. **Makes 4 dozen.**

Note: If using the Food Preparation System, mix sugar, butter, etc., with the stirrer at speed No. 3 and use dough hook when flour has been added at speed No. 3 or No. 4.

Banana Nut Bread

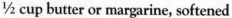

A long time favorite which you can always count on to make mouths water.

½ cup butter or margarine, softened
1 cup sugar
2 eggs
1 large banana, mashed
2 cups all-purpose flour
1 teaspoon baking powder
1 teaspoon baking soda
½ teaspoon salt
1 tablespoon buttermilk powder*
3 tablespoons water
1 cup chopped nuts

Combine butter, sugar, eggs and banana in mixing bowl and beat until light and fluffy. Mix dry ingredients and stir with water into egg mixture just to blend. Fold in chopped nuts. Spoon into a lightly greased non-stick 9 x 5 x 3-inch loaf pan. Bake at 350° F. for 50 to 60 minutes or until a toothpick inserted in center comes out clean. Let bread cool in pan on rack 10 to 15 minutes. Remove from pan and cool on rack. Do not cut bread until completely cool. To store, wrap in aluminum foil. If bread is not to be used within a day or two, refrigerate or freeze. **Makes 1 loaf.**

Note: Use bowl and stirrer of Food Preparation System. Use speed No. 3 to beat butter mixture and speed No. 2 to mix.

*Omit buttermilk powder and water and substitute 3 tablespoons buttermilk, if desired.

Lemon Glazed Plum Bread

Something different to have with morning coffee.

3 firm ripe fresh California plums
2 cups all-purpose flour
2½ teaspoons baking powder
1 teaspoon salt
¼ cup butter or margarine
¾ cup sugar
1 teaspoon grated lemon peel
2 large eggs
1 tablespoon toasted sesame seeds
Lemon glaze

Pit and finely dice plums to measure 1 cup. Mix flour with baking powder and salt. Cream butter with sugar and lemon peel until fluffy. Beat in eggs one at a time. Blend in flour mixture alternately with plums. Stir in sesame seeds. Spoon into a well-greased 7-inch tube pan. Bake at 350° F. for 50 to 55 minutes or until a toothpick comes out clean. Let stand in pan on rack for 10 minutes. Turn out onto wire rack and let stand 10 minutes longer. Set rack over flat pan and brush top of bread with lemon glaze. Cool bread before cutting. **Makes 8 to 10 servings.**

Lemon Glaze: Stir together 2 tablespoons sugar and 1 tablespoon lemon juice.

Note: If you use Food Preparation System, use stirrer in bowl at speed No. 3 for creaming and beating in eggs. Use speed No. 1 for addition of the flour mixture and plums.

Zucchini Bread

A cake-like bread which makes wonderful bread and butter tea sandwiches.

2 eggs
1 cup sugar
½ cup vegetable oil
½ teaspoon vanilla extract
1¾ cups all-purpose flour
¾ teaspoon baking soda
½ teaspoon baking powder
½ teaspoon cinnamon
½ teaspoon salt
1 cup unpeeled grated raw zucchini
½ cup chopped walnuts
½ cup raisins

Beat eggs until very light, about 5 minutes. Slowly beat in sugar, then oil and vanilla. Mix together flour, soda, baking powder, cinnamon and salt. Add alternately to egg mixture with zucchini. Fold in nuts and raisins. Spoon into a non-stick 9 x 5 x 3-inch loaf pan, lightly greased. Bake at 350° F. for 60 minutes or until a toothpick inserted in center comes out clean. Cool in pan on rack for 10 minutes. Remove from pan and cool on rack. When cool, wrap in plastic or aluminum foil. **Makes 1 loaf.**

Note: If using the Food Preparation System slicer/shredder, grate zucchini on blade No. 4 and beat eggs, etc. in bowl with whisk at speed No. 3. Fold in dry ingredients and zucchini with a spatula.

Blueberry Coffee Cake

Delicious hot or cold.

¼ cup butter or margarine
¾ cup sugar
1 egg
½ teaspoon vanilla extract
2 cups all-purpose flour
2 teaspoons baking powder
½ teaspoon salt
½ cup milk
2 cups blueberries, fresh or frozen defrosted
Topping:
¼ cup butter or margarine, softened
½ cup sugar
⅓ cup all-purpose flour

Beat together ¼ cup butter, ¾ cup sugar, egg and vanilla until light and fluffy. Mix 2 cups flour with baking powder and salt and add to sugar mixture alternately with milk, beginning and ending with flour. Fold in blueberries and spoon into a non-stick 9 x 9 x 2-inch pan.

Topping:
¼ cup butter or margarine, softened
½ cup sugar
⅓ cup all-purpose flour

Mix together softened butter, ½ cup sugar and ⅓ cup flour until crumbly and sprinkle over batter in pan. Bake at 375° F. for 35 to 40 minutes or until a toothpick inserted in center comes out clean. **Makes 6 to 8 servings.**

Note: If using the Food Preparation System, use stirrer at speed No. 3 to cream butter and sugar mixture. Add milk and dry ingredients on speed No. 1 and fold in blueberries by hand.

Crunchy Muffins

Muffins to make for breakfast, lunch or dinner.
The cereal included in the recipe provides the crunch.

1½ cups all-purpose flour
3 tablespoons sugar
3 teaspoons baking powder
½ teaspoon salt
1 egg
1 cup milk
3 tablespoons vegetable oil
¾ cup Grape Nuts cereal
½ cup raisins

Mix flour, sugar, baking powder and salt in a bowl. Combine egg, milk and oil and beat well. Add to flour mixture and mix only enough to moisten flour. Fold in cereal and raisins. Fill greased 2½-inch non-stick muffin pans two thirds full or use paper liners in regular muffin pans. Bake at 400° F. for 20 to 25 minutes. **Makes 9 large muffins.**

Orange Coffee Cake

Welcome at breakfast or mid-morning coffee.

2 cups all-purpose flour
4 teaspoons baking powder
½ teaspoon salt
3 tablespoons sugar
4 tablespoons shortening
2 eggs
¾ cup orange juice
¼ cup butter or margarine
¼ cup sugar
1 cup dry bread or cake crumbs
1 teaspoon cinnamon

Mix together flour, baking powder, salt and 3 tablespoons sugar. Cut in shortening with 2 knives or a pastry blender. Beat eggs and add with orange juice, stirring just to blend. Spoon batter into a lightly greased non-stick 9x9x2-inch baking pan. Cream butter and ¼ cup sugar together. Mix in crumbs and cinnamon and sprinkle over top of batter. Bake at 400° F. for 25 to 30 minutes. Cut into squares and serve warm. **Makes 9 servings.**

Corn Muffins

These corn muffins have a couple of surprise ingredients.

1 egg
1¼ cups milk
3 tablespoons vegetable oil
1½ cups all-purpose flour
3½ teaspoons baking powder
1 teaspoon salt
1 tablespoon sugar
1 cup yellow corn meal
1 cup drained whole kernel corn
1 small hot pepper, seeded and finely chopped

Beat together egg, milk and oil. Mix dry ingredients. Combine liquid and dry ingredients, stirring just to blend. Fold in corn and peppers. Fill non-stick muffin pans a little more than ⅔ full. Bake at 400° F. for 25 minutes. **Makes 1½ dozen 2½-inch muffins.**

Date Bran Muffins

These tempting muffins can be reheated or cut and toasted if any are leftover.

¼ cup molasses
2 tablespoons oil
1 egg
1 cup All Bran cereal
¾ cup milk
1 cup all-purpose flour
2½ teaspoons baking powder
½ teaspoon salt
½ cup diced, pitted dates

Beat together molasses, oil and egg. Stir in bran and milk and let stand until milk is absorbed, about 10 minutes.

Mix together flour, baking powder and salt. Stir into bran mixture until just blended. Fold in dates. Fill non-stick muffin pans a little over ⅔ full. Bake at 400° F. for 25 to 30 minutes. **Makes 16 muffins 2½-inches in size.**

Pancakes

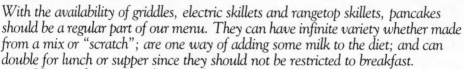

With the availability of griddles, electric skillets and rangetop skillets, pancakes should be a regular part of our menu. They can have infinite variety whether made from a mix or "scratch"; are one way of adding some milk to the diet; and can double for lunch or supper since they should not be restricted to breakfast.

Here is a basic recipe for pancakes. Substitute 1½ cups pancake mix prepared as directed instead of this recipe, if you like.

1¼ cups all-purpose flour
3 teaspoons baking powder
1 tablespoon sugar
¼ teaspoon salt
1 egg
1 cup milk
2 tablespoons vegetable oil

Mix dry ingredients in a bowl. Beat together egg, milk and oil. Stir into dry ingredients just until moistened. Bake on the electric griddle or skillet, preheated at 350° F., turning to brown both sides. When the bubbles in the pancake batter break and the top begins to look slightly dry, it is time to turn the pancake. At the proper temperature a pancake generally takes about 3 minutes to bake altogether. **Makes about 8 (4-inch) cakes.**

Changes:

Blueberry Pancakes: Add 1 cup blueberries which have been allowed to stand with two tablespoons of sugar for 5 minutes. (Use either fresh or frozen, defrosted, blueberries.)

Apple Pancakes: Add 1 cup chopped, peeled apples mixed with two tablespoons of sugar and ⅛ teaspoon cinnamon. Let stand for 5 minutes.

Banana Pancakes: Thinly slice 1 medium ripe banana and fold into batter. Serve with hot honey and butter.

Pecan Pancakes: Add ½ to ¾ cup chopped pecans to basic batter. Stir batter from bottom each time it is added to the grill or skillet.

Clam Pancakes

This is a good way to stretch some clams.

½ cup coarsely chopped clams*
1 ½ cups all-purpose flour
3 ½ teaspoons baking powder
⅛ teaspoon salt
1 egg
Clam liquor plus milk to make 1 cup
¼ cup vegetable oil
2 tablespoons chopped parsley
½ teaspoon grated onion

Cook clams in their own liquid for 2 minutes. Drain liquid and measure.
Mix flour, baking powder and salt in a bowl. Beat together egg, clam liquor and milk and oil. Mix lightly with dry ingredients. Fold in clams, parsley and onion. Bake at 350° F. on preheated griddle, lightly greasing, if necessary. **Makes about 9 (4-inch) pancakes.**

* Canned, chopped clams may be used.

Rice Pancakes

Serve these pancakes with buttered blueberry sauce.

1 cup all-purpose flour
2 teaspoons baking powder
2 tablespoons sugar
¾ teaspoon salt
1 cup milk
2 egg yolks
2 tablespoons vegetable oil
1 cup cooked rice
2 egg whites, stiffly beaten

Mix together flour, baking powder, sugar and salt in a bowl.

Combine milk, egg yolks and oil and beat well. Fold into dry ingredients just until moistened. Fold in rice and beaten egg whites. Bake on a 350° F. preheated griddle. Serve with hot buttered blueberry sauce. **Makes about 8 (4-inch) pancakes.**

Buttered Blueberry Sauce

A fruity flavor to add to the rice pancakes.

2½ tablespoons cornstarch
½ cup sugar
2 cups blueberries, fresh or frozen, defrosted
¾ cup water
3 tablespoons butter

Combine cornstarch and sugar in small saucepan. Stir in blueberries and water. Bring to a boil, stirring constantly. Boil for 3 minutes. Stir in butter. Serve hot with rice pancakes. **Makes about 2 cups.**

Chapter 6

Meat, Poultry, Fish and Beans

There are so many wonderful ways to prepare these important foods in our diet. This chapter has a variety of methods and makes good use of equipment such as the slow cooker, the wok, and the electric skillet to assure excellent results.

Super Steak

These flavors enhance a steak like you wouldn't believe. But be sure to use grated fresh ginger.

3 pounds London broil steak, about 1½-inches thick
¼ cup soy sauce
¼ cup sherry wine
3 tablespoons vegetable oil
1 clove garlic, pressed
1 teaspoon grated fresh ginger

Trim fat and gristle from steak and place steak in a flat glass or enamel pan.

Combine remaining ingredients and pour over steak. Marinate in refrigerator, turning steak often, for at least 2 hours. Broil 4 inches from source of heat for about 8 minutes on each side for medium done. Slice thinly to serve. **Makes 6 to 8 servings.**

Pot Roast with Wine

A well-flavored pot roast to serve with parslied potatoes, steamed green beans and a mixed green salad.

3 to 4 pounds boneless beef pot roast
3 tablespoons all-purpose flour
½ teaspoon salt
Freshly ground pepper to taste
2 tablespoons vegetable oil
1 large onion, chopped
¼ cup tomato paste
½ cup Chianti wine

Rub pot roast with flour which has been mixed with salt and pepper. Heat oil in slow cooker pot and brown roast on all sides over medium heat. Pour off excess fat and transfer cooker pot to heating base, using hot pads. Add onion. Mix tomato paste with wine and pour over meat. Cover and slow cook 6 hours on setting No. 3.

When pot roast is done, remove from slow cooker pot and keep hot. Skim off excess fat from liquid and reduce liquid over high heat to about 1 cup. Slice pot roast and serve with sauce. **Makes 6 to 8 servings.**

Basic Pot Roast

A good basic pot roast recipe is invaluable. You can be pretty sure people will enjoy it, whether family or company. For a change, try the variations suggested.

3 to 4 pounds boneless pot roast
1 clove garlic, cut in half
¼ cup all-purpose flour
½ teaspoon salt
Freshly ground pepper to taste
¼ cup vegetable oil
1 large onion, sliced
1 cup dry white wine

Rub pot roast all over with cut side of garlic clove. Discard garlic. Mix together flour, salt and pepper and rub into pot roast. Heat oil in electric skillet to 350° F. and brown meat on all sides. Pour off accumulated fat from skillet and insert a trivet or rack under the meat in skillet. Add onion and wine. Cover with vent closed and cook meat at "simmer" setting 2½ to 3 hours or until fork tender. Remove meat to platter and keep warm.

    To make gravy: Remove trivet from skillet. Either measure or estimate amount of liquid in pan. Mix together 3 tablespoons flour with water to make 2½ cups total liquid and stir into pan liquid. Using a whisk, cook and stir until mixture boils and is thickened. Taste and add additional salt and pepper if necessary. Slice pot roast and serve with gravy. **Makes 6 to 8 servings**

Variation:
Thirty minutes before end of cooking time, add to skillet potatoes and sliced carrots sufficient for each diner. Remove with meat when making gravy.

Herbed Pot Roast: Make a bouquet garni of ½ bay leaf, ½ teaspoon each thyme and rosemary and several parsley sprigs. Remove before making gravy.

Mushroom Pot Roast: Sauté ¼ pound chopped fresh mushrooms at same time as meat is browning. Do not remove mushrooms while making gravy.

Buffet Meat Loaf

An unusual meat loaf which will grace a hot dinner or a cold buffet equally well.

6 slices thick sliced bacon
4 eggs
1¾ pounds lean ground beef
2 tablespoons chopped fresh chives
¼ cup chopped fresh parsley
1 clove garlic, pressed
½ teaspoon salt
1 teaspoon Worcestershire sauce
¼ pound ground cooked ham
¼ cup dry bread crumbs
4 tablespoons red wine

In a non-stick 9 x 5 x 3-inch loaf pan arrange bacon slices, stretching so they hang over the edge of the pan.

Hard cook two eggs.

Mix 1 raw egg with beef, chives, parsley, garlic, salt, and Worcestershire sauce until well blended. Lightly pack half of the mixture into loaf pan lined with bacon.

Mix remaining raw egg with ham, crumbs, wine and 2 hard-cooked eggs finely chopped. Layer on top of beef mixture in pan and top with remaining beef mixture. Bring bacon slices up over top of meat. Bake at 350° F. for 1½ hours. With a spatula, remove loaf from pan to a platter. Let stand 10 minutes before slicing.

This Buffet Meat Loaf is delicious served hot or cold. To serve cold, chill and slice into thin slices. **Makes 6 servings.**

Note: Fat and juice left in pan may be saved to use for gravy for another meal.

Easy Meatballs with Spaghetti

These meatballs are quickly assembled. A tossed green salad and fresh fruit would complete the meal.

1 pound ground beef
½ cup Italian style bread crumbs
1 egg
2 tablespoons water, if needed
1 tablespoon vegetable oil
1 clove garlic, minced
1 large onion, diced
2 medium fresh tomatoes, peeled and diced
1 can (10½ ounces) beef gravy
½ cup dry red wine
1 pound spaghetti, cooked

Mix ground beef with bread crumbs, egg and water if meatballs seem a little dry. Shape into 16 meatballs.

Put oil in the electric skillet and heat to 350° F. Brown meatballs carefully and remove to another pan as browned. When all are browned, add garlic and onion to skillet and sauté until tender but not browned. Add tomatoes, gravy and wine and bring to a boil. Return meatballs to skillet. Season to taste. Cover, with vent closed, reduce heat to simmer and cook for 30 to 45 minutes. Serve with hot cooked spaghetti. **Makes 4 servings.**

Sukiyaki

This is an Americanized version of a Japanese dish. With an electric wok it can be cooked in front of guests. In advance arrange meat and vegetables on a tray and learn to become proficient with chopsticks to add to the show.

1½ pounds beef steak
2 thinly sliced onions
1 green pepper, seeded and cut in thin strips
1 cup celery, diagonally cut in thin strips
1 can (10 to 12 ounces) bamboo shoots, thinly sliced
1 cup fresh mushrooms, thinly sliced
4 green onions, cut in 1-inch pieces including tops
¼ cup soy sauce
¼ cup sherry wine
2 tablespoons cornstarch
2 tablespoons peanut or vegetable oil
Hot cooked rice

Put the steak in the freezer for one hour and then cut in thin diagonal slices, 2 x 1-inch.

Prepare all the vegetables as directed and arrange on a tray or in bowls.

Mix soy sauce, sherry and cornstarch.

Heat oil in electric wok at 350° F. or in rangetop wok over medium-high heat until very hot. Add meat and onion slices and stir-fry for 1 to 2 minutes until meat loses its red color. Push meat up the side of the wok toward you and add remaining vegetables. Cook and stir quickly for 3 to 4 minutes. Mix meat into vegetables. Stir in soy sauce mixture and stir-fry 1 minute. Serve at once with rice. **Makes 6 servings.**

Stuffed Cubed Steaks

Bake potatoes and tiny whole carrots in lemon juice and butter at the same time as the steaks.

1 cup white bread cubes
¼ pound breakfast sausage
⅔ cup chopped onion
⅔ cup chopped celery and leaves
1 egg
¼ teaspoon salt
Freshly ground pepper to taste
1¼ pounds cubed steaks
2 tablespoons vegetable oil
½ cup beef bouillon

Mix together bread, sausage, onion, celery, egg, salt and pepper. Divide steak into 4 servings and put a portion of the stuffing on each steak. Roll and fasten with skewer or toothpick. Heat oil in skillet over medium heat and brown beef on both sides. Transfer to a casserole and add bouillon. Bake at 350° F., covered, for 1 hour or until meat is tender. **Makes 4 servings.**

Hurry-Up Casserole

Keep the ingredients on hand for this quickly prepared super casserole.

3 cups corn chips
1 large onion, chopped
1 cup grated American cheese
1 can (19 ounces) or 2½ cups chili

Arrange in layers in a 2-quart buttered casserole, 2 cups corn chips, chopped onion and half the grated cheese. Cover with chili and top with remaining corn chips and grated cheese. Bake at 350° F. for 15 to 20 minutes or until bubbling hot. **Makes 6 servings.**

Beef and Vegetables for One

Nothing is easier to prepare for a solo meal than a wok-cooked dish. Go through the vegetable hydrator and use whatever is there that suits your fancy. Our recipe is just a guide, not written in stone.

1 large garlic clove
1 medium onion
½ cucumber
1 stalk celery
1 stalk broccoli
2 to 3 ounces beef steak
1 tablespoon cornstarch
2 tablespoons water
2 tablespoons soy sauce
3 tablespoons sherry
1½ tablespoons vegetable oil
Cooked rice

Chop garlic very fine. Slice onion crosswise into thin slices. Peel cucumber and cut into julienne sticks about 2 inches long. Wash celery and cut on bias into thin strips. Cut broccoli into thin pieces including flower. If much of stem is used, it is best to peel it before slicing. Cut beef into thin slices. Mix cornstarch with water, soy sauce and sherry.

Heat oil in electric wok at 375° F. or in rangetop wok over medium high heat for 2 minutes. Add garlic and stir-fry 1 minute. Add vegetables and stir-fry for 2 minutes. Push vegetables up the side of the wok nearest you and add meat. Stir-fry 2 minutes. Combine vegetables and meat. Add cornstarch mixture, stirring in quickly. When mixture boils, remove from heat and serve at once with rice. **Makes 1 serving.**

Liver Bogata

While liver isn't always the most favorite family food, this South American recipe can convert resisters and it's good eating to boot.

¾ pound beef liver
¼ cup chopped onion
½ green pepper, seeded, chopped
3 tablespoons butter or margarine
2 cups stewed tomatoes
1 stalk celery, chopped
1 small garlic clove, chopped
1 teaspoon salt
Freshly ground pepper to taste
2 tablespoons all-purpose flour
4 tablespoons water
2 cups uncooked egg noodles

Cube liver and sauté with onion and pepper in butter until browned in a 6-cup (1½-quart) saucepan. When brown, add tomatoes, celery, garlic, salt and freshly ground pepper to taste. Bring to a boil, cover and simmer for 30 minutes. Mix flour with water and stir into liver mixture, boiling until thickened. Serve with noodles, cooked as directed. **Makes 4 servings.**

Liver Patties

A tasty way to cook up a little leftover liver.

1 cup leftover ground cooked liver
1 cup leftover mashed potatoes
1 small onion, ground
1 teaspoon Worcestershire sauce
1 egg
½ cup fine, dry bread crumbs
4 tablespoons bacon fat or margarine
1 can (10¼ ounces) beef gravy, if desired or Chili sauce

Mix liver with potatoes, onion, Worcestershire and egg. Shape into 4 patties and dip in bread crumbs. Heat bacon fat in skillet and cook over medium heat, turning to brown both sides. If desired, serve with gravy or chili sauce.

Note: The grinder of the Food Preparation System can be used to grind the liver and onion.

Pork and Bean Sprouts

The electric skillet cooks this combination to perfection.

1 pound raw pork
2 tablespoons vegetable oil
1 cup sliced mushrooms
1 cup sliced onion
1 can (10½ ounces) beef or chicken gravy
1 cup bean sprouts
Salt and freshly ground pepper to taste
Hot cooked rice

Cut pork into thin strips. Heat oil in electric skillet to 350° F. and sauté pork until lightly browned, stirring. Add mushrooms and onion and continue cooking for 5 minutes, stirring. Add gravy, reduce heat to "simmer," cover with vent closed and cook for about 1 hour or until pork is tender. Stir in bean sprouts, season to taste with salt and pepper and serve at once with rice. **Makes 3 to 4 servings.**

Barbecue Spareribs

The perennial favorite.

2 tablespoons butter or margarine
2 cloves garlic, minced
1 large onion, finely chopped
½ cup cider vinegar
¼ cup water
1 can (8 ounces) tomato sauce
3 tablespoons lemon juice
2 teaspoons dry mustard
1½ tablespoons chili powder
Freshly ground black pepper to taste
2 tablespoons sugar
1 bay leaf, finely cut
3 pounds pork spareribs

Heat butter in saucepan and sauté garlic and onion until tender, not browned. Add remaining ingredients except spareribs and simmer, covered, for 15 minutes. Meanwhile cut spareribs between ribs and arrange on a rack in a non-stick 15½ x 10½ x 1-inch baking pan. Bake at 425° F. for 30 minutes. Reduce heat and bake at 350° F. for 1 hour. Baste ribs every 10 to 15 minutes with sauce. Ribs should be browned and crusty. **Makes 4 servings.**

Peanut Butter Monte Cristo

A true Monte Cristo has ham and cheese. As you can see, this is a variation.

2 eggs
¼ teaspoon salt
½ cup milk
12 slices bread
Softened butter
½ cup peanut butter
6 slices baked or boiled ham
¼ cup butter
Jelly

Beat eggs, salt and milk in a flat pan just enough to blend.
　　Make six sandwiches using softened butter, peanut butter and ham slices. Cut in half diagonally. Heat butter on griddle at 350° F. Dip sandwiches in egg mixture and fry on griddle until nicely browned, turning to brown both sides. Serve hot with jelly. **Makes 6 sandwiches.**

Pork Chop Casserole

Serve with baked or mashed potatoes and a green vegetable of your choice. Bake apples for dessert at the same time pork is baking.

4 thin pork chops
1 can (10¾ ounces) golden mushroom soup
1 orange, peeled and sliced

Trim fat from pork chops and fry in skillet until enough fat is released to brown chops. (If the pork chops are lean, use 1 tablespoon butter or margarine.) Brown lightly on both sides and transfer to a small buttered casserole. Heat soup in skillet, scraping any brown crust from pan. Pour over and around pork chops. Top each chop with a thick orange slice. Bake, covered, at 375° F. for 45 minutes or until fork tender. **Makes 2 to 4 servings, depending on appetites.**

Ham Steak with Stuffing

Use your electric skillet to prepare a mustard stuffing with ham steak.

2 tablespoons butter or margarine
¼ cup finely diced celery
¼ cup finely diced onion
2 cups stale bread cubes
2 tablespoons prepared brown mustard
1 teaspoon prepared horseradish
1½ tablespoons brown sugar
1 egg, if desired
2 ham steaks (1 pound each)

Heat butter in a 10-inch skillet and sauté celery and onion over low heat for about 10 minutes, stirring occasionally. Add bread cubes and continue sautéeing, stirring, until bread is lightly toasted. Remove from heat. Stir in mustard, horseradish and sugar until well blended. This makes a dry stuffing. If a moist stuffing is preferred, lightly beat egg and stir into crumb mixture.

Trim off any excess fat from edges of ham and score edges (cut into edge about ½-inch) to keep ham slice from curling. Brown one side of each slice in skillet at 350° F. Place one slice, brown side down in skillet, cover with stuffing and top with other ham slice brown side up. Cover skillet, with vent closed, reduce heat to "simmer" and cook 30 to 40 minutes. To serve, carve through both slices of ham and stuffing. **Makes 6 servings.**

Veal and Noodles

Tossed greens and hard rolls make a good menu with the veal.

1½ pounds veal for stew
¼ cup all-purpose flour
½ teaspoon salt
¼ teaspoon paprika
Freshly ground pepper to taste
2 tablespoons butter or margarine
1 can (13¾ ounces) chicken broth
½ cup pimiento stuffed olives, sliced
3 cups cooked egg noodles, drained

Dredge veal with flour mixed with salt, paprika and pepper. Brown in butter in skillet at 325° F. If any flour does not cling to meat, add to skillet now. Stir in chicken broth and simmer veal, covered, with vent closed, about 45 minutes or until fork tender. Stir in olives and noodles and simmer uncovered to heat through. **Makes 4 to 6 servings.**

Lamb Patties

If you are hungry for lamb but can't afford a leg, try lamb patties. Your Food Preparation System makes it easy to grind your own lamb from some of the less expensive cuts.

6 single soda crackers
1 small clove garlic
¼ teaspoon dried leaf thyme
1 whole clove
½ teaspoon salt
1 egg
2 tablespoons water
1 pound ground raw lamb
1 tablespoon butter or margarine

Grind crackers in your Food Preparation System grinder. Add seasonings and mix well with egg and water in a bowl. Let stand a few minutes until crackers are soft, then lightly mix in lamb. Shape into 4 patties and fry in butter over medium heat about 8 minutes turning to brown both sides. **Makes 4 patties.**

Skillet Barbecued Lamb Steaks with Peaches

A special combination of flavors and perfect for the electric skillet.

6 shoulder lamb steaks
2 tablespoons vegetable oil
1 onion, chopped
1½ cups tomato sauce
½ cup vinegar
¼ cup water
3 tablespoons brown sugar
1 tablespoon Worcestershire sauce
1 teaspoon salt
6 fresh peaches, peeled and sliced
Cooked rice

In electric skillet brown steaks in oil on both sides at 325° F. Remove steaks. Add onion and cook until soft. Add tomato sauce, vinegar, water, sugar, Worcestershire sauce and salt. Return steaks to skillet, spooning sauce over steaks. Bring to a boil, reduce heat to "simmer," cover with vent closed and simmer about 1 hour or until steaks are tender. Add peaches and simmer 5 minutes more. Serve with cooked rice. **Makes 6 servings.**

Chicken Hato Rey

This chicken has a tangy flavor; is juicy inside and is crisp glazed brown on the outside. It's extra special. Serve with ourso*, sliced ripe tomatoes, black olives and Italian bread.

1 broiler-fryer, about 3 pounds
4 teaspoons lime rind
3 tablespoons lime juice
½ cup white rum
½ cup soy sauce
¼ cup dry white wine

Cut broiler into serving pieces, reserving bony pieces for broth. Combine remaining ingredients and marinate chicken in mixture for several hours or overnight in refrigerator.

Remove chicken from marinade and broil, 3 inches from source of heat about 25 minutes, turning pieces to cook and brown on all sides and baste with marinade. **Makes 4 servings.**

* or hot cooked spaghetti

Easy Skillet Chicken Breasts

If you are caught with only frozen chicken breasts and need a tasty dish in a hurry, these chicken breasts will cook while you are busy with the rest of the dinner.

4 frozen chicken breast halves without wings
¼ cup butter or margarine
½ teaspoon seasoned salt
2 garlic cloves, cut in half
½ to 1 cup dry white wine
½ teaspoon dry rosemary leaves, crushed
1½ bay leaves

Separate chicken breast pieces. Heat butter in electric skillet to 350° F. and brown chicken on both sides. Sprinkle with seasoned salt. Add garlic, wine, rosemary and bay leaves. Cover with vent closed and lower heat to "simmer" and cook until chicken is defrosted, turning once or twice. Continue cooking until meat is tender, adding additional wine if necesary. This takes about 45 minutes. Remove garlic and bay leaves and raise heat to 250° F. and reduce liquid to about ⅓ cup. Pour over chicken to serve. **Makes 4 servings.**

Chicken and Asparagus

Nice for luncheon or supper when asparagus is in season, or use frozen cooked asparagus.

4 cups soft bread crumbs
1 cup grated cheddar cheese
½ cup melted butter or margarine
2 cups cooked 1-inch pieces of asparagus
1 can (10¾ ounces) cream of chicken soup
1 soup can milk
2 cups cooked, diced chicken*

Mix together bread crumbs, cheese and melted butter. Spread half the mixture into a lightly buttered, non-stick 9 x 9 x 2-inch baking pan. Put asparagus in a layer on crumbs. Mix soup with milk and heat to boiling. Add chicken and pour over asparagus. Sprinkle with remaining crumb mixture. Bake at 350° F. about 30 minutes until bubbly and browned. **Makes 4 to 6 servings.**

* Cooked turkey, veal or shrimp may be substituted for chicken.

Chicken Macaroni Skillet Dinner

Quickly prepared. Serve with lettuce wedges topped with a tart dresssing and heated hard rolls.

2 cups cooked, coarsely diced chicken
1 cup chopped onion
1 can (about 10½ ounces) condensed cheddar cheese soup
1 can (8 ounces) tomatoes
½ teaspoon crushed dried rosemary
2 cups cooked elbow macaroni
Grated Parmesan cheese

Combine chicken with onion, soup, tomatoes, rosemary and macaroni. Heat in skillet over low heat about 10 minutes or until flavors are blended, stirring occasionally. Serve with Parmesan cheese. **Makes 4 servings.**

Sweet and Sour Chicken Nuggets

This makes a very good buffet dish.

Vegetable oil
½ cup buttermilk pancake mix
1 can (10¾ ounces) condensed chicken broth
1 pound boneless chicken cut in 1-inch chunks (about 2 cups)

Fill electric skillet 1-inch deep with oil and heat to 375° F. Combine pancake mix with ¼ cup chicken broth. (Reserve remaining broth.) Add chicken to pancake mixture and stir until all pieces of chicken are coated. Fry 10 to 12 pieces at a time in hot oil, 3 to 4 minutes or until crisp and golden brown. Remove with slotted fork and drain on absorbent paper. Place chicken on rack in shallow baking pan and keep hot in a 300° F. oven while preparing sauce. **Makes 6 servings.**

Sweet and Sour Sauce

1 large green pepper, cut in strips
½ cup chopped onion
1 can (8 ounces) pineapple chunks in unsweetened juice
2 tablespoons cornstarch
½ cup maple flavored syrup
¼ cup vinegar
1 tablespoon soy sauce
1 medium tomato, seeded and coarsely chopped
3 cups hot rice

Pour off all but 2 tablespoons oil from skillet. Sauté green pepper and onion in remaining oil until tender crisp. Drain pineapple, reserving ¼ cup juice. Combine ¼ cup juice with cornstarch. Combine remaining chicken broth, syrup, vinegar and soy sauce. Add to vegetable mixture and bring to a boil. Stir in cornstarch. Simmer 1 minute until thickened and clear, stirring. Add pineapple and heat. Just before serving add chicken and tomato. Serve over hot cooked rice.

Braised Cornish Game Hens Madeira

An electric skillet with a high dome lid is perfect for braising Cornish game hens.

4 fresh Cornish game hens
Salt and freshly ground pepper
3 tablespoons olive oil
1 large onion, thinly sliced
2 cloves garlic, finely minced
1 tablespoon flour
½ cup dry white wine or vermouth
½ cup chicken broth
2 tomatoes peeled and chopped
2 tablespoons tomato paste
½ teaspoon oregano
¼ cup green olives, seeded and chopped

Pat hens dry and season inside and out with salt and pepper. Fold wings back and tie legs together. Heat olive oil in electric skillet to 350° F. and brown hens on breasts. Remove to another dish.

Reduce heat slightly and sauté onion and garlic for 5 minutes. Stir in flour. Add remaining ingredients and season with salt and pepper to taste. Place hens in skillet, breast side up, and bring to a boil. Reduce to "simmer," cover with vent closed and simmer for 45 minutes or until tender. **Makes 4 servings.**

Turkey, Pepper, Wok Style

The bright green of the peppers and red of the tomatoes makes this pretty as well as tasty.

4 small Italian peppers
1 medium onion
3 Italian tomatoes, coarsely chopped
1 package (1 pound) turkey breast cutlets
¾ cup chicken bouillon
1 tablespoon cornstarch
2 tablespoons peanut or vegetable oil
Salt and freshly ground pepper to taste
Hot cooked rice

Seed and cut peppers into about 2-inch squares. Cut onion in half lengthwise and then into thin slices crosswise. Coarsely chop tomatoes. Cut turkey cutlets into thin strips. Mix bouillon with cornstarch.

Heat oil in electric wok at 375° F. or large sauté pan over medium high heat for about 2 minutes. Add vegetables and stir-fry for 3 or 4 minutes. The peppers should still be crisp. Push vegetables to side of wok next to you and add turkey. Stir-fry until turkey meat turns white. Mix with vegetables. Add bouillon mixture and bring to a boil, adding salt and pepper to taste. Serve at once with cooked rice. **Makes 4 servings.**

Stuffed Turkey Breast

Boning the breast is a little trouble, but once you master it you'll enjoy a wonderful recipe.

1 turkey breast, 4½ to 5 pounds
½ cup butter or margarine
1 medium onion, chopped
1 stalk celery, chopped
¼ cup chopped fresh parsley
1 cup chopped fresh mushrooms
½ teaspoon powdered dried thyme
½ teaspoon salt
Freshly ground pepper to taste
2 large slices white bread
1 egg
½ cup dry white wine

Carefully bone the turkey breast so that it can be stuffed.

Heat ¼ cup butter in large skillet and sauté onion, celery, parsley, and mushrooms until tender. Add thyme, salt and pepper. Cut bread into small cubes and stir into vegetables until well blended. Remove from heat and cool. Stir in egg and spoon into turkey breast. Hold together with string or skewers.

Heat remaining ¼ cup butter in electric skillet to 325° F. and brown turkey breast on all sides. Add wine to skillet, cover, with vent closed, reduce heat to "simmer" and cook until turkey meat is fork tender, 1½ to 2 hours. Slice to serve. **Makes 6 servings.**

Note: Freeze turkey bones for soup at a later date.

Picnic Beans

When time is limited, put together these beans for the picnic. They'll be a hit.

4 slices bacon, chopped
1 onion, chopped
1 green pepper, seeded and diced
½ cup molasses
1 tablespoon prepared brown mustard
2 cans (1 pound each) baked beans, any style

Fry bacon and onion together until bacon is crisp. Add remaining ingredients and mix lightly. Spoon into a non-stick 9 x 9 x 2-inch pan and bake at 350° F. about 45 minutes. **Makes 6 servings.**

Lima Bean Bake

A substantial main dish which can be prepared in the oven or in a slow cooker.

1 pound dried large lima beans
6 cups water
6 slices bacon, cut up
2 cups chopped onion
1½ cups bean liquid
2 chicken bouillon cubes
1 sprig or ¼ teaspoon dried summer savory
Salt and freshly ground pepper to taste

Wash beans and place in a large saucepan. Add water and soak overnight.
Next day bring beans to a boil and simmer 1 hour.
Meanwhile, fry bacon until crisp and remove from skillet and reserve. Fry onion in bacon fat until tender, not browned. Combine drained beans, onion, enough bean liquid to cover beans, bouillon cubes, summer savory, bacon, salt and pepper in a 10-cup (2½-quart) casserole. Bake at 325° F. for 2 hours or until beans are tender and liquid thickens. (If necessary, however, add more bean liquid.) **Makes 6 servings.**

Note: This lima bean bake can be cooked in the slow cooker for 8 to 10 hours on setting No. 2.

Brown Beans

These brown beans are found on smorgasbords, or served with meat balls.

2 cups dried brown or pinto beans
1 teaspoon salt
1 tablespoon vinegar
1 tablespoon sugar
2 tablespoons molasses

Wash beans, cover with water about 2 inches above beans and soak overnight in slow cooker pot. Next morning add salt, vinegar, sugar and molasses. Cook on setting No. 3 for 6 to 8 hours. Check several times to see if additional liquid is needed. Season to taste. **Makes 4 servings.**

Piquant Navy Beans

These beans will go well with ham, hot dogs, pork chops or even scrambled eggs.

1 pound dried navy beans
Water to cover
1 teaspoon salt
2 teaspoons dry mustard
2 teaspoons sugar
¼ cup bacon drippings or margarine
2 tablespoons lemon juice

Pick over and wash navy beans well. Cover with water about 2 inches above the beans and soak overnight. Next morning add salt and cook beans until just tender, about 1½ hours. Let the bean liquid cook down toward the end of the cooking time. Mix mustard, sugar, bacon drippings and lemon juice with a little of the bean liquid and return to beans and lightly mix together. Heat well. Will keep covered in the refrigerator for about a week. **Makes 10-12 servings.**

Note: This dish may be prepared in the slow cooker. Soak washed beans overnight in cooker pot. Next morning cook beans on No. 2 for 5 to 6 hours. Add seasonings about 1 hour before beans are done.

Rice and Shrimp

A pleasing one dish meal combination. Serve with lettuce wedges and crusty bread.

3 tablespoons butter or margarine
1 medium onion, chopped
½ medium green pepper, seeded and chopped
1 can (4 ounces) sliced mushrooms and liquid
3 cups tomato juice
1 cup regular uncooked rice
½ cup chopped stuffed olives
1½ cups shrimp, canned or fresh
Salt and freshly ground pepper to taste

Heat butter in electric skillet to 350° F. and sauté onion and pepper until tender, about 5 minutes, stirring. Add mushrooms, tomato juice, rice and olives and stir. Cover with vent closed and cook at "simmer" for about 25 minutes. Stir two or three times. Mix in shrimp and continue cooking until shrimp is heated, about 10 minutes. Season to taste. **Makes 4 servings.**

Sole with Fresh Tomato Sauce

Fish fillets at their best. Serve with new potatoes, broccoli, and crusty Italian bread.

5 tablespoons butter or margarine
4 cups chopped fresh tomatoes
½ teaspoon dried tarragon leaves
1 medium onion, finely chopped
Freshly ground pepper to taste
½ cup all-purpose flour
½ teaspoon salt
2 pounds sole or flounder fillets

Heat 1 tablespoon butter in a saucepan. Add tomatoes, tarragon, onion and pepper. Bring to a boil, cover and cook over low heat for about 5 minutes. Keep hot.

Mix flour with salt. Dip fish fillets in mixture. Heat 4 tablespoons butter to 325° F. in the electric skillet and fry fillets quickly, turning to brown both sides. If necessary add more butter. Serve with tomato sauce. **Makes 4 to 6 servings.**

Fish and Potato Casserole

You can prepare and refrigerate this casserole in advance, ready to bake at serving time.

¼ cup water
2 teaspoons dried onion flakes
2 cooked medium potatoes
1 can (10¾ ounces) cream of mushroom soup
1 can (4 ounces) mushroom stems and pieces, undrained
½ teaspoon Angostura bitters
2 tablespoons white wine
¾ pound boneless white fish fillets
½ cup bread crumbs
2 tablespoons butter or margarine

Mix water with onion flakes and let stand 10 minutes. Peel and slice potatoes. Blend onions, soup, mushrooms and liquid, bitters and wine.

Layer half potatoes and half fish in buttered flat 1½ to 2-quart casserole. Pour over half soup mixture. Repeat with remaining ingredients. Sprinkle crumbs on top of fish and dot with butter. Bake at 400° F. for 30 minutes. **Makes 4 servings.**

Fish and Chips

A happy way to cook fish.

1 cup all-purpose flour
1 teaspoon baking powder
½ teaspoon salt
1 egg, slightly beaten
⅔ cup milk
1 tablespoon corn oil
1½ pounds fish fillets
Corn oil
Potato chips or French fries

Combine flour, baking powder and salt in a bowl. Mix egg, milk and 1 tablespoon oil, add to flour mixture and stir until smooth. Cut fish in serving size or smaller pieces and dip in batter. Fill electric skillet about half full of oil and heat to 375° F. Fry 3 or 4 fillets at one time, turning to brown on all sides. Should take no more than 3 to 4 minutes. Drain on paper towels. Repeat frying remaining fish. Serve hot with potato chips or French fries. **Makes 4 servings.**

Baked Fish au Gratin

A combination of fish and cheese which stretches the servings.

1 pound white fish fillets
8 slices American cheese
¼ cup chopped fresh parsley
¼ cup corn oil
1 cup chopped onion
2 tablespoons cornstarch
⅛ teaspoon salt
Freshly ground pepper to taste
¼ cup sherry
1¼ cups milk
½ cup buttered bread crumbs

Butter a flat 1½ to 2-quart casserole and layer fillets and cheese slices alternately with cheese on top layer. Sprinkle with parsley. Heat oil in skillet and sauté onion until tender, not browned. Stir in cornstarch, salt and pepper and remove from heat. Slowly stir in sherry and milk. Return to heat and bring to a boil, stirring constantly. Boil 2 minutes. Pour over fish and cheese. Bake at 400° F. for 20 minutes. Sprinkle with buttered crumbs and bake 10 minutes longer. **Makes 4 servings.**

Fish Roll Ups

An easy-to-do fish dish.

1 medium onion, sliced
1 can (7 ounces) tuna, flaked
½ cup finely chopped celery
1 pound flounder or sole fillets
½ cup real mayonnaise
⅓ cup dairy sour cream
3 tablespoons chili sauce

Line bottom of a buttered flat 1½ to 2-quart casserole with onion slices. Mix tuna fish and celery. Divide tuna mixture evenly over fillets and roll. Place on top of onion slices. Mix together mayonnaise, sour cream and chili sauce. Pour over fish. Bake at 325° F. for 25 minutes or until fish flakes easily. **Makes 4 servings.**

Crab Meat Supreme

A fabulous dish that needs only steamed fresh asparagus, Apple Cole Slaw (page 97) and Light 'n Lovely Lemon Pie (page 123) to complete the meal.

4 tablespoons butter or margarine
1 tablespoon chopped green pepper
½ teaspoon Dijon-style mustard
¼ teaspoon paprika
½ teaspoon salt
4 tablespoons all-purpose flour
1 cup milk
2 teaspoons capers
1 teaspoon Worcestershire sauce
1 pound crab meat
1 egg yolk
6 tablespoons mayonnaise

Heat butter in 2-quart saucepan over medium heat, and sauté green pepper 2 minutes. Add mustard, paprika, salt and flour, and cook 2 minutes. Add milk and stir while cooking until mixture comes to a boil and is thickened. Fold in capers and Worcestershire sauce. Shred crab meat and remove any spines. Add with egg yolk and mayonnaise to sauce. Spoon into a buttered shallow casserole. Bake at 400° F. for 25 to 30 minutes, or until bubbly. **Makes 4 servings.**

Chapter 7

Vegetables and Salads

Here is a harvest of exciting vegetables to be cooked, steamed, stir-fried, sautéed or baked. Interesting flavor combinations and herbs and spices give you a whole new world of vegetable cookery. Crisp salads add a different flavor and texture to menus, and should be a part of each day's meal plans. Stainless steel bowls are perfect for preparation and refrigerator storage of salads.

Wok Cooked Vegetables

Stir-frying

The beauty of the stir-fry method of cooking vegetables in the wok is that any combination that suits your taste can be used. If the vegetables are long cookers such as carrots, cut them into smaller pieces, or stir-fry them for a few minutes before other vegetables are added. The only thing to remember is that all necessary preparation must be done before cooking is started. Here are some combinations to get your imagination going.

Celery, green beans, cabbage, garlic
Cauliflower, carrots, green onions
Cherry tomatoes, fresh herbs and chopped parsley
Italian peppers, celery, onions, garlic
Julienned turnips, onions, celery
Shredded raw spinach, pinenuts
Broccoli, mushrooms, onions
Sliced raw asparagus and mushrooms
Eggplant, onion, chopped fresh tomatoes, chopped fresh basil
Bell peppers, chopped tomatoes, onions
Snow peas, mushrooms

General directions include preparing vegetables in thin slices or julienne strips. Heat about 1 tablespoon peanut or vegetable oil in electric wok at 350-375° F. or rangetop wok over moderate heat about 2 minutes. Add longest cooking vegetables and stir-fry 1 to 2 minutes. Add remaining vegetables and stir-fry 2 minutes more. A combination of cornstarch, sherry and soy sauce may be added or the vegetables may be seasoned to taste with salt and pepper.

Steaming

Besides its use for stir-fry cooking, the wok is great for steaming. If you are into Chinese cooking the wok can be used to steam *dim sum* in one of its many variations (one facet of Chinese cooking) or for steamed stuffed buns and dumplings from the northern part of China, plus many other delicious items.

A metal rack can be used for steaming vegetables in the wok. Add water to wok just below the rack and bring to a boil, covered. Almost any vegetable which grows and is normally eaten hot can be steamed. The flavor and vitamins are retained and a superior product results. If you are cooking for a small family, several vegetables can be steamed in the wok at the same time. For example, put potatoes in first and arrange them at one side of the rack. Then add whatever other vegetables you are having in time for them to steam tender crisp. Butter, lemon juice or other seasonings can be added after the vegetables are cooked. Combinations of vegetables can be steamed together, such as green beans and chopped onions, or lima beans and chopped celery or cabbage and carrots.

Count on less cooking time for vegetables being steamed.

Bean Sprouts

A necessity for any wok cooking and marvelous in salads.

To make your own bean sprouts, wash ⅓ cup mung beans and soak overnight in a quart glass canning jar. Next morning drain beans and cover jar with a piece of cheesecloth held on by a ring jar cover. Rinse and drain the beans in cool water several times a day, right through the cheesecloth. They will start sprouting almost immediately and by the third day the bean sprouts should fill the jar.

To store, cover sprouts with cold water and store in the refrigerator. The bean sprouts will keep crisp and ready for use for as long as they last, at least several weeks.

If you use lots of bean sprouts, keep 2 jars going. When the bean sprouts are half gone, start a new batch.

Note: A ring jar cover is a canning jar screw top with no center.

Broccoli and Bean Sprouts

A delicious vegetable combination which will complement any meal.

1 pound (about) fresh broccoli
2 tablespoons peanut or vegetable oil
½ cup thinly sliced onion
2 tablespoons water
1 tablespoon soy sauce
1 cup bean sprouts

Trim off outer leaves and tough ends of broccoli. Cut stalks and flowers into thin slices. Heat oil in electric wok at 375° F. or in range top wok over medium-high heat about 1 minute. Add broccoli and onion and stir-fry until broccoli is bright green. Add water and soy sauce and heat to boiling. Cover and steam 1 to 2 minutes. Stir in bean sprouts and heat 1 minute. Serve at once. **Makes 4 servings.**

Turnip/Carrot Combination

You might like to serve this dish with any meat or fish.

1 medium white turnip
2 carrots
1 small onion
2 tablespoons butter or margarine
3 to 4 tablespoons water
Freshly ground pepper to taste

Peel turnip and carrots and thinly slice. Slice onion. Combine in a small saucepan. Add remaining ingredients. Bring to a boil, reduce heat and simmer, covered, 10 minutes. Check to see if additional water is needed during cooking. **Makes 4 servings.**

Braised Cabbage and Bacon

A dish for the electric skillet. Serve with new boiled potatoes, a green salad and rye bread.

1 medium-small head cabbage
8 slices bacon, diced
1 medium onion
3 carrots
1 stalk celery, sliced
2 tablespoons chopped fresh parsley
1 teaspoon chopped fresh basil
1 package instant chicken bouillon
½ cup water
Freshly ground pepper to taste

Trim cabbage and cut into 4 wedges. Remove core. Put about 1 cup water in an electric skillet and set temperature to 250° F. Add cabbage wedges, cover and steam cabbage for 5 minutes. Remove to a plate and drain water from skillet.

Fry bacon at 350° F. until almost done. Drain off fat. Meanwhile, halve and slice onion thinly, peel and cut carrots into thin slices. Add with cabbage and remaining ingredients to skillet. Cover, reduce to simmer and cook about 10 minutes longer until cabbage is still tender-crisp. **Makes 4 servings.**

Note: Slicer/Shredder attachment of Food Preparation System may be used to slice onion and carrots with the thin slicing blade (No. 2) and to slice the celery with the thick slicing blade (No. 1).

Chinese Cabbage

Most grocers carry Chinese cabbage these days and it is a perfect partner for the wok.

½ **large Chinese cabbage (Bok Choy)**
3 slices fresh ginger
2 garlic cloves
1 tablespoon peanut or vegetable oil

Remove outer leaves from cabbage and shred cabbage finely. Place in colander and rinse with cold water. Peel and chop ginger. Crush garlic.

Heat oil in electric wok at 325° F. or in rangetop wok over medium heat for 2 minutes. Add ginger and garlic and stir-fry 2 minutes. Do not brown. Add cabbage; stir and toss to mix with garlic and ginger and coat with oil. Cover and cook 3 to 4 minutes. Cabbage should still be crisp. **Makes 4 to 6 servings.**

Leeks Australian

Leeks are a vegetable not used enough in this country. They are a delicious relative of the onion family.

4 medium-sized leeks
2 hard-cooked eggs
8 tablespoons mayonnaise
Finely chopped fresh parsley

Trim off green tops of leeks so leeks are about 6 inches long. (The tops can be refrigerated to use in soup making if they are in good condition.) Cut leeks in half lengthwise and rinse under running water to remove sand between folds.

Boil leeks in salted water 12 minutes or until tender. Meanwhile, peel eggs. Put yolks through strainer and chop whites.

When leeks are tender, rinse in cold water and drain. Allow to cool. Put two halves on each plate, top with mayonnaise and sprinkle with egg yolks, whites and parsley. **Makes 4 servings.**

Baked Onion Dumplings

These flavorful dumplings could be baked along with chicken or a roast.

2 cups sliced Spanish onions
2 tablespoons butter or margarine
¼ teaspoon salt
Freshly ground pepper to taste
½ cup dairy sour cream
1 egg, beaten
½ teaspoon dried thyme, basil or dill
2 cups buttermilk biscuit mix
⅔ cup milk

Heat butter in a 10-inch skillet and sauté onions until golden. Season and reserve. Mix sour cream, egg and herb. Lightly combine biscuit mix and milk and spread on bottom of a non-stick 9 x 9 x 2-inch baking pan. Spread cooked onions on top. Spoon cream mixture over onions. Bake at 400° F. for 20 minutes or until topping is set and starting to brown. Cut in squares and serve warm. **Makes 9 servings.**

Rice Pilaf with Cumin

Bake this rice casserole while a roast or other meat or fish dish is in the oven.

½ cup chopped onion
¼ cup chopped green pepper
1 cup uncooked rice
2 tablespoons bacon fat or oil
2 cups boiling beef broth or consommé
1 tablespoon Worcestershire sauce
¾ teaspoon cumin seed
Salt to taste

Sauté onion, green pepper and rice in bacon fat over low heat in a small skillet until rice is golden brown, stirring. Spoon into an 8 cup (2-quart) shallow casserole and stir in remaining ingredients. Cover tightly with lid or foil and bake at 350° F. for 30 minutes or until rice is tender and liquid is absorbed. Before serving fluff rice with fork. **Makes 6 servings.**

Mincemeat Rice

Serve as an accompaniment to meat or poultry. It will be one of the stars of your dinner.

½ cup chopped onion
¼ cup chopped celery
2 tablespoons butter or margarine
3 cups cooked rice
⅔ cup brandied mincemeat*

In saucepan, sauté onion and celery in butter until tender. Add rice and mincemeat. Blend and heat thoroughly. **Makes about 4 cups or 6 servings.**

*Or use ⅔ cup regular mincemeat and 2 tablespoons brandy.

Potato Cakes

Make these special potato cakes "planovers" by preparing extra potatoes.

1 cup chopped onion
2 tablespoons butter or margarine
2 cups cold mashed potatoes
3 tablespoons all-purpose flour
Salt and freshly ground pepper to taste
1 egg
1 tablespoon water
½ cup corn meal
2 tablespoons vegetable oil

In saucepan, sauté onion in 1 tablespoon butter until tender. Mix with potatoes, flour, salt and pepper to taste. Shape into 6 patties about an inch thick. Mix egg with water and dip potato cakes in mixture and then in corn meal. Heat remaining butter and oil in a large skillet over medium heat and brown potato cakes on both sides, about 5 to 6 minutes. **Makes 6 potato cakes.**

Herbed Potato Puff

You can prepare this recipe up to the point of baking and keep it refrigerated until about 40 minutes before serving time. You'll need to bake it 35 or 40 minutes instead of the suggested 20 minutes.

3 large potatoes
4 tablespoons butter or margarine
2 tablespoons all-purpose flour
3 tablespoons grated onion
1 tablespoon minced parsley
¼ teaspoon chopped rosemary leaves
1 teaspoon garlic salt
½ teaspoon salt
1 egg
6 tablespoons milk (about)

Peel and boil potatoes until tender. Drain and mash. In the mixing bowl of your Food Preparation System, with the stirrer on speed No. 3, mix potatoes with other ingredients. Beat until light and fluffy. If more milk seems indicated, add a little at a time until mixture is soft, but not runny. Spoon into a non-stick 9 x 9 x 2-inch baking pan and bake at 375° F. for 20 minutes. **Makes 4 servings.**

Stir-fry Vegetable Combination

A mixture of vegetables that goes well with broiled chicken or fish. Serve with steamed rice and thinly sliced whole wheat bread.

1 tablespoon cornstarch
3 tablespoons soy sauce
¼ cup dry sherry or bouillon
2 tablespoons peanut or vegetable oil
1½ cups thinly sliced celery
1½ cups thinly sliced seeded Italian peppers
5 stalks raw asparagus, sliced on bias
1 cup bean sprouts

Mix cornstarch, soy sauce and sherry and set aside.

Heat oil in electric wok at 375° F. or in rangetop wok over moderate heat for 2 minutes. Add celery, peppers and asparagus and stir-fry for 2 minutes. Add bean sprouts and stir-fry for 1 minute longer. Stir in cornstarch mixture and when it boils and is thickened serve vegetables at once. **Makes 4 servings.**

Asparagus Polonaise

Asparagus, a favorite spring vegetable, livens up any meal.

1 to 1½ pounds fresh asparagus
½ cup dry bread crumbs
⅓ cup butter or margarine
1½ tablespoons lemon juice
Salt and freshly ground pepper to taste

Snap off tough ends of asparagus and wash asparagus well. Steam until tender crisp, about 5 to 8 minutes, in the wok.

Meanwhile, combine bread crumbs and butter in a small skillet and cook and stir until crumbs are lightly browned. Stir in lemon juice and seasonings. Put steamed asparagus in serving dish and sprinkle with crumbs. **Makes 4 to 5 servings.**

Scalloped Green Beans and Celery

A special vegetable casserole that goes well with most meats.

1 pound fresh green beans
1 cup diced celery
½ teaspoon salt
1 can (10¾ ounces) cream of tomato soup
½ cup grated American cheese
½ cup soft bread crumbs
¼ cup melted butter or margarine

Cook green beans and celery in saucepan with lightly salted water until just tender. Drain and layer in a buttered flat 1½ to 2-quart casserole. Cover with tomato soup and sprinkle with cheese. Mix bread crumbs with butter and sprinkle over cheese. Bake at 350° F. for about 30 minutes or until bubbly and browned. **Makes 6 servings.**

Artichoke Casserole

Serve this artichoke casserole as a main course for a light luncheon.

4 artichokes
½ lemon
½ cup cottage cheese
½ cup chopped, cooked ham
2 tablespoons finely chopped onion
1 egg
2 tablespoons chopped fresh parsley
1½ tablespoons lemon juice
½ teaspoon salt
Freshly ground pepper to taste
¾ cup buttered bread crumbs
½ cup (about) chicken broth

Trim stems and tops of artichokes and cut in half lengthwise. Remove and discard choke and wash artichokes well. Cover with water in a saucepan, add half lemon and cook, covered, 20 to 25 minutes or until almost tender. Drain, cut side down.

Combine cheese, ham, onion, egg, parsley, lemon juice, salt and pepper with half the bread crumbs and enough chicken broth to moisten.

Place artichoke halves cut side up in a buttered shallow baking dish. Spoon cheese mixture on artichokes, mounding toward center. Sprinkle with remaining buttered crumbs. Pour any remaining chicken broth in bottom of casserole. Bake at 375° F. for 30 minutes or until lightly browned.
Makes 4 servings.

Succotash

A modern version of succotash, a dish we inherited from the Indians.

3 cups fresh green beans
3 cups fresh corn cut from the cob
3 tablespoons butter or margarine
½ cup rich milk or light cream
Salt and freshly ground pepper to taste

Steam beans in the wok until tender, about 10 minutes. Add corn and steam 1 or 2 minutes longer. Heat butter and milk together in saucepan and combine with beans and corn. Add salt and pepper to taste. Serve at once.
Makes 4 to 6 servings.

Ratatouille

A French vegetable combination to be served hot or cold. Cold, it is an excellent salad accompaniment to cold cuts.

⅓ cup olive or vegetable oil
2 small onions, thinly sliced
2 small green peppers, seeded and thinly sliced
1 or 2 cloves garlic, minced
1 medium eggplant (about 1 pound), cut in small chunks
2 medium zucchini (about ¾ pound), thinly sliced
2 ripe tomatoes, thinly sliced
Salt and oregano to taste

Heat oil in large skillet or saucepan. Sauté onions and green peppers with garlic over low heat until vegetables are limp. Remove from skillet and add eggplant and zucchini (both unpeeled) to pan. Sauté, stirring up from bottom until slightly softened. Add tomatoes, salt, oregano, onions and green peppers. Cover and simmer for about 30 minutes, stirring occasionally. **Makes 4 to 6 servings.**

Green and Yellow Squash

Mixing these two colors makes a pretty vegetable combination.

2 medium zucchini squash
2 medium yellow summer squash
2 green onions
1 to 2 tablespoons freshly chopped parsley
Freshly ground pepper to taste
2 to 3 tablespoons water
2 tablespoons butter or margarine

Scrub squash clean and unless essential do not peel either. Slice thinly. Slice onion crosswise, using both green and white part. Combine with squash, parsley, pepper, water and butter in a small saucepan. (Vegetables should always be cooked in a pan small enough so that it is ⅔ full of the vegetables being cooked.) Bring to a boil, reduce heat and simmer covered over low heat about 5 minutes or just until tender crisp. **Makes 4 servings.**

Pumpkin Fritters

Serve these as a vegetable side dish or as the main course of a light meal.

2 large or 3 small eggs
⅔ cup sugar
1½ cups all-purpose flour
¼ teaspoon salt
1 teaspoon nutmeg
¾ teaspoon cinnamon
1 cup steamed pumpkin*
1 teaspoon vanilla extract
1 teaspoon baking powder
¼ to ½ cup melted butter or margarine

Beat eggs well in the mixing bowl of your Food Preparation System with the stirrer on speed No. 3. Mix sugar and flour with salt and spices. Reduce to speed No. 2 and fold mixture into eggs. Beat until smooth and fluffy. Add pumpkin, vanilla and baking powder. Heat butter in a large skillet or griddle set at 350° F. Drop by tablespoonfuls into heated butter. Cook slowly, turning to brown both sides. Repeat until all batter is used. **Makes about 2 dozen fritters.**

* Canned pumpkin may be used.

Barley Casserole

Barley is one of our best casseroles. Serve it often.

⅓ cup regular barley
½ teaspoon salt
2 cups boiling water
1 package (10 ounces) frozen chopped spinach, thawed
1 can (10¾ ounces) condensed tomato soup
1 cup fresh mushroom slices
½ cup chopped onion
½ teaspoon garlic salt
Freshly ground pepper to taste
2 tablespoons butter or margarine

Stir barley and salt into boiling water in a saucepan. Reduce heat and simmer, covered, about 20 minutes. Drain barley. Drain liquid from spinach and add with soup, mushrooms, onion, garlic salt, pepper and butter to barley. Spoon into a buttered 8 or 9-inch square baking dish. Bake at 350°F. for about 30 minutes or until hot. **Makes 4 servings.**

Lettuce and Tomato Salad with
Creamy Buttermilk Dressing

This dressing is a healthy combination of ingredients suitable for both fruit and vegetable salads.

Dressing:
2 cups cottage cheese
1 cup buttermilk
1 tablespoon red wine vinegar
2 tablespoons chopped parsley
¾ teaspoon seasoned salt

In the blender of the Food Preparation System, whir cottage cheese on speed No. 3 or 4 until very smooth. Add buttermilk, wine vinegar, parsley and salt and blend on No. 2 until well mixed. This **makes 3 cups** dressing and will keep for about 2 weeks if stored covered in the refrigerator.

Wedges of crisp lettuce
Sliced red onion
Thinly sliced tomatoes

To make a salad, arrange a crisp wedge of lettuce on a salad plate or bowl, one for each person to be served. Top with onion and tomato slices. Serve with creamy buttermilk dressing.

Cannellini Salad

Good with cold cuts or on an antipasto platter.

1 can (20 ounces) cannellini beans, drained
¼ cup olive oil
2 tablespoons lemon juice
¼ teaspoon salt
Freshly ground pepper to taste
3 green onions, thinly sliced
1 ripe tomato, peeled, seeded and chopped

Combine drained beans with remaining ingredients. Chill. Serve without lettuce. **Makes 4 servings.**

Summer Salad

A colorful addition to a meal.

1 cup shredded leaf lettuce
2 ripe tomatoes, chopped
3 green onions chopped, both green and white parts
1 cucumber, peeled, seeded and chopped
8 radishes, thinly sliced
¼ cup chopped fresh parsley
1 teaspoon chopped Summer Savory
⅓ cup olive oil
2 tablespoons wine vinegar
Salt and freshly ground pepper to taste

Combine vegetables in salad bowl. Mix together olive oil, vinegar, salt and pepper. Toss lightly with vegetables. Serve at once. **Makes 4 servings.**

Green Bean Salad

A crisp salad-relish to add to the menu.

2 packages (10 ounces each) frozen French-style green beans
2 tomatoes
1 green onion
1 cup thinly sliced celery
¼ cup (about) oil and vinegar dressing
Crisp lettuce, if desired

Cook beans in saucepan as directed on package and chill in ice water. Drain very well. Peel tomatoes, slice thinly and remove seeds and cut slices into quarters. Thinly slice both white and green part of onion. Combine vegetables with oil and vinegar dresssing and chill several hours. If desired, serve on lettuce. **Makes 6 servings.**

Apple Cole Slaw

A variation of that old favorite, cole slaw.

1 wedge cabbage, trimmed
1 crisp apple, peeled and cored
1 carrot, peeled
1 small onion, peeled
½ cup dairy sour cream
2 tablespoons cider vinegar
Salt to taste

Put cabbage, apple and carrot through the fine slicer blade (No. 2) of the slicer/shredder attachment of the Food Preparation System or in a food processor use the steel blade. Mix vegetables with cream, vinegar and salt to taste. Chill. **Makes 4 servings.**

Macaroni Salad

A wonderful salad for a buffet. It can be prepared in advance and kept chilled until ready to serve.

4 cups cooked small macaroni shells
2 cups peeled and diced tomatoes
¾ cup finely diced, seeded green peppers
½ cup finely diced celery
3 tablespoons finely chopped stuffed olives
2 tablespoons chopped fresh parsley
½ cup chopped green onions, tops and bottoms
1 cup mayonnaise
1 tablespoon Worcestershire sauce
1 tablespoon wine vinegar
1 teaspoon salt
Crisp lettuce, if desired

In a large bowl combine macaroni shells, tomatoes, peppers, celery, olives, parsley and green onions. Cover and chill.

Mix mayonnaise with remaining ingredients except lettuce, and add to macaroni about 30 minutes before serving. Toss well. Serve on crisp lettuce, if desired. **Makes 8 to 10 servings.**

Mixed Vegetable Salad

This salad is perfect for winter. You could substitute frozen vegetables.

2 cans (16 ounces each) mixed vegetables
½ cup sliced celery
½ cup Spanish onion, coarsely chopped
6 tablespoons vegetable oil
3 tablespoons tarragon vinegar
1½ teaspoons Worcestershire sauce
¾ teaspoon salt
Freshly ground pepper to taste

Drain vegetables and mix well with remaining ingredients. Chill several hours or overnight, stirring vegetables occasionally. Serve as a salad or a relish. **Makes about 4 cups.**

Broccoli Salad

For a pleasant change, serve broccoli as a salad instead of a hot vegetable.

½ head crisp raw broccoli
4 tablespoons pickle relish
2 green onions, chopped
1 hard-cooked egg, chopped
1 tablespoon lemon juice
¼ cup mayonnaise
Salt and freshly ground pepper to taste
Crisp lettuce

Wash and dice broccoli into ½-inch cubes. (Peel tender part of stems and use them in the salad also.) There should be about 2 cups. Put in a bowl and mix with pickle relish, onions, hard cooked egg, lemon juice and toss with mayonnaise, adding additional if necessary. Taste and add salt and pepper if desired. Chill well. Serve in lettuce cups. **Makes 4 servings.**

Red Potato Salad

A tart potato salad. Good with hot or cold meats.

6 medium red potatoes
4 tablespoons dry white wine
1 clove garlic
1 teaspoon Dijon mustard
3 tablespoons tarragon vinegar
½ cup vegetable oil
1 green onion, cut up
2 or 3 sprigs parsley
Salt and freshly ground pepper to taste

Scrub potatoes well and cook in boiling salted water until just tender, about 15 minutes. Drain, dice and put in a bowl. Pour wine over potatoes. Cover and let cool to room temperature.

In the blender of the Food Preparation System, combine garlic, mustard, vinegar, vegetable oil, green onion and parsley. Spin in blender at speed No. 3 until parsley and onion are finely cut. Pour over potatoes in bowl. Mix lightly and add salt and pepper to taste. Chill for about an hour. **Makes 4 servings.**

Chinese Chicken Salad

Give your luncheon an Oriental theme. Serve with thin-sliced bread and butter sandwiches and garnish salad with mandarin oranges.

¼ cup soy sauce
2 teaspoons prepared mustard
1 tablespoon vegetable oil
2½ cups cooked chicken, cut in thin strips
3 cups cooled cooked rice
1 cup sliced green onions, including tops
Salt and freshly ground pepper to taste
Shredded lettuce
Mayonnaise
1 can (3 ounces) Chow Mein noodles or rice noodles

Combine soy sauce, mustard and oil. Add chicken or other meat and toss lightly. Allow to marinate at least 1 hour. Stir in rice and onions and add salt and pepper to taste. Chill. To serve, spoon onto beds of shredded lettuce. Top with mayonnaise and sprinkle generously with Chow Mein noodles. **Makes 6 servings.**

Note: You may substitute cooked beef or pork.

Peanut and Carrot Salad

A salad the kids will like.

2 cups finely chopped carrots or 3 large carrots
1 cup chopped salted peanuts
1 tablespoon grated onion or 1 small onion
1 tablespoon lemon juice
⅓ cup mayonnaise
Crisp lettuce
Dill pickle

The vegetables can be prepared using the coarse shredding blade (No. 3) of the Food Preparation System slicer/shredder.

   Put processed carrots, peanuts and onion in a bowl and add lemon juice and mayonnaise. Serve on crisp lettuce garnished with a dill pickle slice. **Makes 4 servings.**

Fresh Fruit Salad

Arrange orange sections, sliced fresh pears, peaches, grapes or whatever fruits are in season on shredded lettuce.

Dressing:
½ cup salad oil
¼ cup vinegar
½ teaspoon salt
¼ teaspoon paprika
¼ teaspoon nutmeg
1 medium banana, peeled and diced
1 teaspoon lemon juice
1 tablespoon sugar

Combine all ingredients in blender. Cover and blend until smooth. Chill well. Serve with fruit salad. Do not count on this dressing for more than 2 days storage, covered, in the refrigerator. **Makes about 1¼ cups.**

Note: Use blender of Food Preparation System at speed No. 3.

Chapter 8

Egg and Cheese Dishes

Eggs and cheese are enjoyable on their own, or when mixed with a number of other foods, We've included combinations with pastas, vegetables, seafood and other delicious ingredients.

Since eggs and cheese require low heat cookery for best results, temperature controlled equipment such as electric skillets, griddles and Silver-Stone® lined cookware that respond to range temperatures insure success.

Remember in cheese and egg cookery, for casseroles or other oven-baked dishes, to preheat the oven to the proper temperature.

Stuffed Pasta Shells with Anchovy Sauce

These pasta shells can be stuffed, refrigerated, and heated with sauce when ready to serve. It is a choice dish.

Anchovy Sauce:

1 clove garlic, finely chopped
2 tablespoons olive oil
2 cans (2 ounces each) anchovy fillets
1 can (6 ounces) tomato paste
2 cups water
¼ teaspoon salt
Freshly ground pepper to taste
1 teaspoon dry basil
2 tablespoons chopped parsley

In large skillet, cook garlic in olive oil for 2 minutes. Chop anchovy fillets and add with their oil to garlic. Stir in remaining ingredients and simmer 10 minutes.

Pasta Shells:

24 large pasta shells (about ½ pound)
1 pound ricotta cheese
1 egg
4 tablespoons freshly grated Parmesan cheese
Salt and freshly ground pepper to taste

Cook pasta shells as directed on package. Drain and cool enough to handle. Mix ricotta cheese with egg, 2 tablespoons Parmesan and salt and pepper to taste. Fill shells with ricotta mixture.

Put a thin layer of sauce in bottom of a non-stick 9 x 9 x 2-inch baking pan. Put stuffed shells into pan in one layer. Top with remaining sauce and sprinkle with remaining 2 tablespoons Parmesan. Bake at 350° F. for about 30 minutes or until bubbly. **Makes 4 servings.**

Vegetable Noodle Bake

A blend of spring vegetables, noodles and cheese. Fresh Fruit Mold (page 127) would be appropriate with this casserole meal.

3 cups uncooked medium egg noodles
1 tablespoon vegetable oil
¼ cup butter or margarine
½ cup chopped onion
2 medium zucchini, sliced
2 fresh tomatoes, peeled and diced
1 cup sliced fresh mushrooms
¼ cup chopped fresh parsley
1 cup ricotta cheese
1 teaspoon dried basil, crushed
½ teaspoon salt
Freshly ground pepper to taste
¼ cup seasoned bread crumbs

Cook noodles as directed on package, slightly al dente. Drain and mix lightly with oil.

Heat butter in skillet and sauté onion until tender. Add zucchini, tomatoes, mushrooms and parsley and cook about 5 minutes longer. Cool slightly and mix in ricotta, basil, salt and pepper.

Arrange a third of noodles in a buttered 6-cup (1½-quart) casserole. Add half of the vegetable mixture and another third of noodles. Spoon in remaining vegetables and top with remaining noodles. Cover and bake at 350° F. for 20 minutes. Uncover, sprinkle on bread crumbs and bake 10 minutes longer or until bubbly. **Makes 4 servings.**

Celery Cheese Casserole

Delicious with roast beef or pork.

4 cups celery, cut in 1-inch slices
1½ cups grated cheddar cheese
1 can (10¾ ounces) cream of mushroom soup
3 tablespoons butter or margarine
⅓ cup chopped salted peanuts

Cook celery in a small amount of boiling water for about 5 minutes. Drain. In a buttered 6 cup (1½-quart) casserole alternate layers of celery, cheese and soup, ending with soup. Dot with butter and sprinkle with peanuts. Bake at 350° F. for 20 minutes or until bubbly. **Makes 4 servings.**

Baked Cheesewiches

Plain sliced tomatoes or a tossed green salad would complement these hot sandwiches for lunch or supper.

3 tablespoons butter or margarine, softened
1 tablespoon brown mustard
8 slices firm bread, cut ½-inch thick
4 slices sharp cheddar cheese
3 eggs
2 cups milk
1 tablespoon chopped fresh chives
1 tablespoon chopped fresh basil
⅛ teaspoon salt

Mix butter with mustard and spread on bread slices. Make sandwiches with cheese. (Use thick slices of cheese.) Fit sandwiches into a non-stick 9 x 9 x 2-inch baking pan. Beat eggs with remaining ingredients and pour over sandwiches in pan. Let stand for 2 hours or overnight. Bake at 350° F. for 1 hour or until browned lightly. **Makes 4 servings.**

Sunday Omelet

A ham and pineapple omelet to serve for lunch, brunch or a late night snack.

1 tablespoon butter or margarine
4 eggs
¼ cup cream or milk
¼ teaspoon salt
Freshly ground pepper to taste
¾ cup flaked cooked ham
½ cup crushed pineapple, well drained
1 teaspoon chopped parsley

Melt butter in a 10-inch sauté pan over medium heat. Beat eggs until very light and fluffy. Gradually beat in cream, salt and pepper. Pour into hot skillet and cook over moderate heat until center is almost set. Combine ham, pineapple and parsley and spread over omelet. Place under broiler for a few minutes to heat filling and set omelet. (Protect handle of skillet by wrapping with aluminum foil, if necessary.) Fold omelet over and serve on warmed platter. **Makes 2 servings.**

Note: This recipe may be doubled and cooked in a 12-inch sauté pan.

Ham 'n Egg Casserole

A complete meal in a dish. Add a green vegetable and hot French bread. Can be prepared in advance, refrigerated and baked when needed.

6 hard-cooked eggs
¼ cup finely chopped celery
1 tablespoon mayonnaise
1 teaspoon prepared mustard
6 slices cooked ham
1 can (10¾ ounces) cream of mushroom soup
⅓ cup milk
½ cup grated cheddar cheese
¼ cup crushed potato chips
Sliced, stuffed olives

Slice eggs in half and remove yolks. Mash yolks, combine with celery, mayonnaise and mustard. Refill whites with yolk mixture and put two halves back together. Wrap each egg in a ham slice, placing it with the fold side down in a 9-inch square baking pan. Combine the mushroom soup and milk and pour over the ham and egg rolls. Sprinkle with grated cheese and crushed potato chips. Top with sliced, stuffed olives. Bake at 350° F. for 30 minutes or until sauce is bubbly. **Makes 6 servings.**

Eggplant Cheese Casserole

A meatless main dish which can be combined with a bean sprout and green onion salad and whole wheat bread.

1 large eggplant
2 eggs, beaten
2 tablespoons water
¾ teaspoon Italian seasoning
1 cup fine dry bread crumbs
½ cup olive or vegetable oil
3 cups tomato sauce
12 ounces sliced mozzarella cheese
2 ounces freshly grated Parmesan cheese

Peel and slice eggplant into thin slices. Beat eggs, water and Italian seasoning together. Dip eggplant in egg mixture then in crumbs and brown in large skillet with oil, adding as needed. Put eggplant as browned in a shallow casserole. Cover first layer with half the tomato sauce, half the mozzarella and Parmesan. As remaining eggplant is browned, repeat layer. Bake at 350° F. for 40 to 50 minutes until bubbly. **Makes 6 servings.**

Shrimp and Egg Bake

Something different for your next brunch party.

6 hard-cooked eggs, peeled and halved lengthwise
1 pound shelled and deveined small shrimp
2 tablespoons butter or margarine
2½ tablespoons all-purpose flour
2 cups milk
½ teaspoon salt
¼ teaspoon paprika
1 teaspoon prepared mustard
Dash steak sauce
1 cup shredded Gouda or Muenster cheese
6 rusks or 3 cups cooked rice

Arrange eggs and shrimp in the bottom of a flat 1½ to 2-quart casserole dish. Melt butter in a saucepan and stir in flour. Let cook about 1 minute. Gradually blend in milk, stirring constantly over medium heat until sauce thickens and boils. Remove from heat and stir in salt, paprika, mustard, steak sauce and cheese. Pour sauce over eggs and shrimp. Bake at 400° F. for 15 minutes or until bubbly. Serve over rusks or cooked rice. **Makes 6 servings.**

Seafood Quiche

A happy thought for any meal.

1 9-inch unbaked pastry shell
2 tablespoons chopped green onions, both white and green
2 tablespoons butter or margarine
1½ cups white fish, shrimp, scallops or any combination
3 eggs, lightly beaten
1½ cups Half and Half
¼ teaspoon salt
Freshly ground pepper to taste
½ teaspoon nutmeg
½ cup grated Swiss cheese
Paprika

Bake pie shell at 400° F. for 7 to 8 minutes. Cool.

In skillet, sauté onions in butter for 5 minutes. Add seafood and cook 2 to 3 minutes more. Combine onion, seafood, eggs, Half and Half, salt, pepper, nutmeg and cheese. Sprinkle with paprika. Pour into partially baked pie shell and bake at 375° F. for 30 to 35 minutes or until custard is set. May be served hot or cold. **Makes 6 servings.**

Potatoes with Cheese Sauce

Tasty and filling. Complete the menu with sliced tomatoes and dill pickles.

5 tablespoons butter or margarine
¼ cup minced onion
½ cup diced celery
5 tablespoons all-purpose flour
1 teaspoon salt
Freshly ground pepper to taste
3½ cups milk
1¼ cups shredded cheddar cheese
5 cups hot mashed potatoes or 4 large baked potatoes
Paprika

Heat butter in a saucepan over medium-low heat and sauté onion and celery until tender but not browned. Stir in flour, salt and pepper and cook one minute. Gradually stir in milk and cook and stir until mixture boils and is thickened. Stir in cheese. Spoon cheese sauce over mashed potatoes or baked potatoes which have been cut and opened out. Sprinkle with paprika. **Makes 4 servings.**

Rice Frittata with Green Chilies

Fried rice with a bit of a bite from the chilies, but oh so good.

½ cup finely chopped onion
1 tablespoon butter or margarine
8 eggs
½ cup milk
1 teaspoon salt
1 teaspoon Worcestershire sauce
4 or 5 drops hot pepper sauce
2 cups cooked rice
1 can (4 ounces) chopped green chilies, undrained
1 medium tomato, chopped
½ cup shredded cheddar cheese

In a 10-inch skillet over medium-high heat cook onions in butter until tender. Beat eggs with milk and seasonings. Stir in rice, chilies, and tomatoes. Pour into skillet and reduce heat to medium low. Cover and cook until top is almost set, 12 to 15 minutes. Sprinkle with cheese. Cover. Remove from heat and let stand 10 minutes. **Makes 4 servings.**

Corn and Egg Scramble

A quick change for breakfast.

¼ pound bacon, diced
2 cups cooked whole kernel corn
4 eggs, lightly beaten
2 tablespoons water
½ teaspoon salt
Freshly ground pepper to taste
½ cup grated American cheese
Hot buttered toast

Sauté bacon in skillet until nicely crisped. Drain corn and add to bacon and stir until corn is hot. Mix eggs with water, salt, pepper and cheese. Add to corn and bacon. Cook and stir over low heat until eggs are set. Serve with hot buttered toast. **Makes 4 servings.**

Baked Noodles and Cottage Cheese

Great for Sunday night supper. A crisp salad and you're all set.

1 package (12 ounces) uncooked medium egg noodles
2 tablespoons salad oil
½ cup chopped onion
¼ cup chopped fresh parsley
½ teaspoon salt
⅛ teaspoon hot pepper sauce
2 cups dairy sour cream
2 cups smooth cottage cheese
½ cup buttered fine bread crumbs

In a large saucepan or Dutch Oven cook noodles as directed until just tender. Drain and mix with salad oil. Combine remaining ingredients except bread crumbs and arrange in alternate layers with noodles in a buttered 9 x 9 x 2-inch baking pan. Sprinkle top with bread crumbs. Bake at 350° F. for 20 to 25 minutes. **Makes 6 servings.**

Chapter 9

Cakes and Cookies

The always popular cake and cookies react to non-stick bakeware like a flower does to sunshine. They bake beautifully in well-constructed baking pans but remember never to use non-stick bakeware at temperatures higher than 425° F. They only need greasing if a product is high in sugar. Remember to preheat the oven and take advantage of your Food Preparation System to take over the mixing.

Spice Cake

Marvelous squares of cake to serve alone or cut a little smaller and serve with fruit for dessert.

1 cup shortening
2 cups sugar
2 eggs
3 cups all-purpose flour
4 teaspoons cocoa
1 teaspoon cinnamon
½ teaspoon allspice
½ teaspoon salt
½ cup cultured buttermilk powder*
2 teaspoons baking soda
2 cups water

Beat together shortening, sugar and eggs until light and fluffy using stirrer of Food Preparation System at speed No. 3. Mix together flour, cocoa, cinnamon, allspice, salt and buttermilk powder. Dissolve soda in water and add alternately with dry ingredients to creamed mixture beginning and ending with dry ingredients. Mix just to blend at speed No. 1. Spoon batter into a lightly greased non-stick 11 x 7-inch baking pan. Bake at 350° F. 40 to 45 minutes or until a toothpick inserted in center comes out clean. Cake may be turned out on a cake rack to frost, or frost in the pan.
Makes 15 servings.

* 2 cups regular buttermilk may be used instead of buttermilk powder and water.

Brown Sugar Frosting: Melt 6 tablespoons butter or margarine in a skillet. Add ½ cup brown sugar and ⅓ cup milk. Bring to a boil and cook 2 minutes. Remove from heat and cool. Beat in 1½ cups sifted confectioners' sugar and ½ teaspoon vanilla extract. Spread over top of spice cake.

Angel Sponge Cake

No leftover egg yolks from this pretty cake.

5 eggs
¾ teaspoon cream of tartar
1½ cups sugar
½ cup cold water
1½ cups all-purpose flour
1 teaspoon baking powder
¼ teaspoon salt
1 teaspoon vanilla extract

To make this cake in the Food Preparation System, separate eggs and put whites into bowl. Beat with whisk at speed No. 4 until foamy. Add cream of tartar and beat until stiff. Gradually beat in ½ cup of the sugar. The whites should be very stiff. Remove whites to another bowl.

    Without washing the bowl, put egg yolks into bowl and beat with whisk at speed No. 4 until thick and lemon colored. Gradually add water while beating and continue beating 4 minutes. Add 1 cup sugar and beat 1 minute longer. Mix flour, baking powder and salt together and add to egg yolk, using speed No. 1. Add vanilla. Remove whisk and fold beaten egg whites into batter with a rubber spatula. Spoon into an ungreased 9-inch angel food cake pan. Bake at 350° F. for 40 minutes or until cracks on top are dry. Invert pan to cool cake. Remove cooled cake from pan and frost with Confectioners' Sugar Icing. **Makes 8 to 10 servings.**

Confectioners' Sugar Icing: Add enough hot water (about 2 tablespoons) to 2 cups sifted confectioners' sugar so it is of a consistency that can be drizzled over the cake. Flavor with 1 teaspoon vanilla extract. It should be a very thin layer, more like a glaze.

Apple Raisin Cake

A moist cake flavorful with apples and spices.

1½ cups all-purpose flour
1 cup sugar
½ cup real mayonnaise
3 tablespoons milk
1 egg
1 teaspoon baking soda
¼ teaspoon salt
¼ teaspoon nutmeg
¾ teaspoon cinnamon
⅛ teaspoon ground cloves
1½ cups chopped, peeled apples
½ cup raisins
¼ cup chopped walnuts

Grease and flour an 8 or 9-inch square pan or use non-stick bakeware.

In a large bowl combine flour, sugar, mayonnaise, milk, egg, soda, salt and spices. Beat at low speed for 2 minutes. Stir in apples, raisins and nuts. Spoon into pan. Bake at 350° F. for 40 minutes. Cool in pan on rack and frost with chocolate frosting. **Makes 16 servings.**

With Food Preparation System, use bowl and stirrer on speed No. 2.

Chocolate Frosting: Sift 2 cups confectioners' sugar. In a small non-stick saucepan melt 2 squares (1 ounce each) chocolate and 2 tablespoons butter or margarine over very low heat. Remove from heat and beat in half the sugar, ½ teaspoon vanilla and 1 tablespoon milk. Continue beating in sugar and adding a tablespoon or two more of milk until frosting can be spread. Spread, while still warm, on cooled cake. Sprinkle with 2 tablespoons finely chopped walnuts.

Bon Bon Pineapple Cake

A delicious cake worthy of any special occasion. Frost with a recipe of your choice, but chocolate is highly recommended.

½ cup shortening
1 cup sugar
3 eggs, separated
2¼ cups all-purpose flour
2 teaspoons baking powder
½ teaspoon salt
1 can (9 ounces) crushed pineapple
½ cup orange juice

Cream shortening, ¾ cup sugar and egg yolks until light and fluffy. Mix dry ingredients together and add alternately with crushed pineapple and orange juice to creamed mixture, beginning and ending with flour mixture.

Beat egg whites until stiff with remaining ¼ cup sugar and fold into batter. Spoon into two lightly greased 9-inch non-stick cake pans. Bake at 350° F. for 25 minutes or until a toothpick inserted in center comes out clean. Remove from pans and cool on rack. **Makes 8 to 10 servings.**

Chocolate Frosting: Cream 6 tablespoons butter and gradually add about half of a one pound package of confectioners' sugar, sifted. Beat in 2 tablespoons coffee cream and 2 squares (1 ounce each) melted and cooled unsweetened chocolate. Continue adding remainder of confectioners' sugar and 2 more tablespoons coffee cream, beating until light and creamy and of spreading consistency. Frost between, on top and sides of pineapple cake.

Note: In the Food Preparation System use the bowl and stirrer and beat on speed No. 3.

Applesauce Cake

An easily prepared dessert from our Scandinavian friends.

4 tablespoons butter or margarine
2 cups zwieback crumbs
½ teaspoon cinnamon
1⅓ cups commercial applesauce
Whipped cream

Melt butter and mix with crumbs and cinnamon and stir in skillet until crumbs are lightly browned.

Layer crumbs and applesauce in a buttered 5-cup (1¼-quart) casserole, starting and ending with crumbs. Bake at 375° F. for 25 to 35 minutes. Chill. Unmold and serve with whipped cream. **Makes 6 servings.**

Rich Drop Cookies

These cookies do the disappearing act in a hurry.

½ cup shortening
1 cup brown sugar, firmly packed
½ cup dairy sour cream
1 egg
1 teaspoon vanilla extract
2 cups all-purpose flour
1 teaspoon nutmeg
½ teaspoon baking soda
2 teaspoons baking powder
½ teaspoon salt
½ cup chopped pecans

Cream together shortening, sugar, sour cream, egg and vanilla until light and fluffy. Mix together dry ingredients and stir into creamed mixture. Fold in nuts. Drop by teaspoons on non-stick cookie sheets and bake at 375° F. for 10 minutes or until edges are lightly browned. Remove from pan to cooling rack at once. **Makes 4 dozen 2-inch cookies.**

Note: With the Food Preparation System, use the mixer bowl and the stirrer on speed No. 3 for creaming and No. 2 for adding dry ingredients.

Double Chocolates

Really, really, tasty cookies. Store in airtight container to keep a crisp outside and soft center.

1 cup shortening
¾ cup brown sugar, firmly packed
1 cup granulated sugar
1 cup skim milk ricotta cheese
2 eggs
1½ teaspoons vanilla extract
2¾ cups all-purpose flour
1 teaspoon baking powder
½ teaspoon baking soda
½ teaspoon salt
½ cup cocoa
½ cup chopped nuts
1 cup chocolate chips
½ cup (about) confectioners' sugar

Combine shortening with brown sugar and granulated sugar, ricotta, eggs and vanilla. Beat at medium to high speed until blended thoroughly. (Mixture will look slightly curdled.) Mix or sift flour with remaining dry ingredients (except confectioners' sugar) and stir into creamed mixture. Fold in nuts and chocolate chips. Chill for 2 hours or overnight.

   To bake, form into small balls and dip in confectioners' sugar. Place on non-stick cookie sheet. Bake at 350° F. for 12 to 15 minutes. **Makes about 6 dozen.**

Note: With the Food Preparation System, use the mixer bowl and the stirrer on speed No. 3 for creaming and No. 2 for adding dry ingredients.

Oatmeal Cookies

This simple combination of ingredients makes a delicate cookie.

3 cups uncooked oatmeal
⅔ cup butter or margarine
½ cup sugar

Put oatmeal, butter and sugar on a clean mixing surface and mix with your hands until well blended. Shape into 50 small balls and put on non-stick cookie sheets at least two inches apart. With fork dipped in water press cookies flat. Bake at 350° F. for 13 to 15 minutes. These cookies flatten and become thin wafers so be sure to allow enough room between cookies on baking sheet. **Makes 50.**

Cream Cheese Cookies

These cookies are not too sweet.

1½ cups all-purpose flour
1½ cups ground oat flour*
¼ teaspoon salt
1 cup butter or margarine, softened
1 package (8 ounces) cream cheese, softened
½ teaspoon vanilla extract
Apricot preserves
Confectioners' sugar

Combine flours and salt in a bowl. In a large bowl combine butter, cream cheese and vanilla and beat until light and fluffy. Add dry ingredients and mix well. Cover and chill about one hour. Roll out half of the dough at a time on lightly floured board to ⅛-inch thickness. Cut with a floured round cookie cutter or other desired shape and place on non-stick cookie sheet. With the back of a half teaspoon measuring spoon, press an indentation in center of each cookie and fill with ½ teaspoon apricot preserves. Bake at 350° F. for about 15 minutes or until edge of cookies are lightly browned. Transfer to rack and sprinkle with confectioners' sugar. **Makes about 4 dozen.**

Note: Use the mixer bowl of the Food Preparation System and the stirrer at speed No. 3 to beat the butter, etc. Add flour mixture with stirrer and use speed No. 1.

* To make 1½ cups oat flour, grind 2 cups of uncooked oatmeal in blender of the Food Preparation System 1 cup at a time until oats are very finely ground.

Cranberry Cookies

These crunchy cookies are an attractive addition to an assortment.

½ cup butter or margarine
1 cup granulated sugar
¾ cup brown sugar, firmly packed
¼ cup milk
2 tablespoons orange juice
1 egg
3 cups all-purpose flour
1 teaspoon baking powder
¼ teaspoon baking soda
¼ teaspoon salt
1 cup chopped nuts
2½ cups cranberries, coarsely chopped

Cream butter and sugars together. Beat in milk, orange juice and egg. Mix flour with baking powder, soda and salt. Combine with creamed mixture and blend well. Stir in nuts and cranberries. Drop by teaspoons on a non-stick cookie sheet. Bake at 375° F. for 10 to 15 minutes. **Makes 12 dozen.**

Cinnamon Cookies

Easy to make and easy to eat.

⅔ cup vegetable oil
1 cup sugar
1 egg
¼ cup honey
2 cups all-purpose flour
2 teaspoons baking soda
1 teaspoon cinnamon
Additional sugar

Beat together oil, 1 cup sugar, egg and honey until light and fluffy. Mix together flour, soda and cinnamon. Add to egg mixture, stirring just to blend. Chill dough 30 minutes. Shape into walnut-size balls and roll in granulated sugar. Bake on lightly greased non-stick cookie sheet at 350° F. for 8 to 10 minutes. **Makes 3½ dozen.**

Brandy Rings

This is a cookie to grace the Christmas cookie scene. They are worth the trouble.

1⅓ cups butter or margarine
¾ cup sugar
3 cups all-purpose flour
3 tablespoons brandy

Mix all ingredients together until a smooth dough is formed. Pinch off about ¼ of the dough. (Keep remaining dough in refrigerator.) Roll on a floured surface with a floured rolling pin to make strips 5-inches wide and about ¼-inch thick. Cut crosswise into thin strips and twist two together to shape into rings. Repeat procedure with remaining dough. Place on a non-stick cookie sheet and bake at 350° F. for 10 to 12 minutes or until cookies are lightly browned. **Makes 75.**

Note: If using Food Preparation System, put ingredients in the bowl, mix with the stirrer at speed No. 1 until blended and speed No. 3 to finish dough.

Chapter 10

Desserts and Pastries

Desserts and pastries are the queens of the meal. When planning to serve a spectacular dessert, make the meal simple. That way your dessert will get the raves it deserves.

Always do any food preparation as far in advance as feasible. An example — a pie shell can always be made and baked the day before it is to be filled.

Learn to pace your kitchen chores so as not to tire yourself more than necessary, and you'll enjoy cooking for your family or guests even more.

Pumpkin Pie Granada

Flavorful with spices, this is a pumpkin pie for special occasions.

Pastry Shell:

Mix together in a small bowl 1¼ cups all-purpose flour, ¼ teaspoon salt, 1½ tablespoons sugar and ¾ teaspoon grated lemon rind. Cut in 7½ tablespoons cold butter with two knives or a pastry blender. Stir in 1 egg yolk with a fork. If necessary, add a few drops of cold water so pastry will cling together. Shape pastry into a flat round cake, wrap in plastic wrap and chill about 30 minutes in refrigerator. Roll on a cloth covered floured board to fit a non-stick 9-inch pie pan. Flute edges.

Filling:

¾ cup dark brown sugar, firmly packed
¾ cup light brown sugar, firmly packed
¼ teaspoon salt
¾ teaspoon cloves
2 teaspoons cinnamon
1 teaspoon ginger
¼ teaspoon allspice
1 can (15 or 16 ounces) pumpkin
Grated rind of 1 lemon
3 eggs
1 can (13 ounces) evaporated milk
2 tablespoons brandy
½ cup chopped pecans

Mix sugars with salt and spices until well blended. Add pumpkin, lemon rind, eggs, evaporated milk and brandy and stir well with a whisk or use Food Preparation System with stirrer at speeds No. 2 or 3. Stir in pecans. Pour into pie shell. Bake at 425° F. for 45 to 50 minutes or until custard is almost set. It will continue to cook after it is removed from the oven. Cool pie before cutting. **Makes 6 to 8 servings.**

Cherry Pie

Not just for George Washington's birthday.

3 tablespoons cornstarch
⅔ cup sugar
¼ teaspoon salt
1 cup juice drained from cherries
2 tablespoons butter or margarine
1 teaspoon lemon juice
¼ teaspoon red food coloring, if desired
2 cans (1 pound each) pitted sour red cherries, packed in water, drained
Pastry for 2 crust pie

Combine cornstarch, sugar, salt and cherry juice in a saucepan. Cook and stir over medium heat until mixture boils and is thickened, then continue boiling for 1 minute. Remove from heat and stir in butter, lemon juice, food coloring and cherries.

Roll out half the pastry and fit into a non-stick 9-inch pie pan. Fill with cherry filling. Roll out remaining pastry and cut into 1-inch strips. Put over filling to form a lattice top. Flute edges. Bake at 425° F. for 35 to 40 minutes until crust is golden. **Makes one 9-inch pie.**

Prune Meringue Pie

A different kind of a prune pie which is delicious.

½ cup sugar
1 tablespoon cornstarch
1 cup stewed prunes, drained, pitted and cut up
3 egg yolks
1 cup evaporated milk
1 teaspoon vanilla extract
1 unbaked 9-inch pie shell
3 egg whites
6 tablespoons sugar

Combine ½ cup sugar, cornstarch, prunes, egg yolks, milk, and vanilla, stirring to blend well. Spoon into unbaked pie shell and bake at 400° F. for about 35 to 40 minutes or until filling is set.

Beat egg whites until very stiff. (You should be able to hold bowl upside down and the egg whites won't fall out.) Fold in 6 tablespoons sugar gradually with a folding motion. Spread over filling, being sure to seal meringue to pie around edges. Bake at 350° F. for 18 minutes. **Makes 6 to 8 servings.**

Note: Use whisk and bowl of Food Preparation System. Beat at speed No. 4.

Sundae Pie

An easy dessert considering its spectacular appearance.

1½ pints vanilla ice cream
1½ pints orange sherbet
1 baked 9-inch pie shell
Chocolate sauce

Alternate scoops of vanilla ice cream and orange sherbet in the pie shell. Store in freezer until ready to serve, at least 6 hours. At serving time spoon chocolate sauce over pie. **Makes 6 to 8 servings.**

Chocolate Sauce: Melt 3 (1 ounce each) squares unsweetened chocolate and ⅔ cup water in a small saucepan. Cook over low heat until well blended, stirring frequently. Add ½ cup sugar, bring to a boil and cook gently 2 minutes. Stir in ½ cup light corn syrup and boil 5 minutes. Cook and add ½ teaspoon vanilla extract. Store, covered, in refrigerator. Can be used hot or cold. **Makes 1½ cups.**

Brownie Pie

A rich dessert. Cut down on the calories someplace else!

2 squares (1 ounce each) unsweetened chocolate
¼ cup butter or margarine
2 eggs
1 cup sugar
1 teaspoon vanilla extract
1 cup buttermilk biscuit mix
1 cup chopped pecans
Ice Cream or Whipped topping

Melt chocolate and butter in a saucepan. Beat eggs until light and gradually beat in sugar and vanilla. Add chocolate and butter and beat well. Fold in biscuit mix and pecans. Spread into a greased non-stick 9-inch pie pan and bake at 350° F. for 20 to 25 minutes. Serve warm or cold with ice cream or whipped topping. **Makes 6 to 8 servings.**

Note: If using beater and bowl of Food Preparation System, beat eggs with whisk on speed No. 4 until light and fluffy. Continue beating on No. 4 while adding sugar and vanilla and chocolate mixture. Reduce speed to No. 2 when adding flour and nuts.

Light 'n Lovely Lemon Pie

A wonderful finish to a meal.

Crust:
4 cups Rice Chex cereal
¼ cup brown sugar, firmly packed
¼ cup chopped pecans
⅓ cup butter or margarine

Crush rice cereal to make 1 cup. Mix with remaining ingredients and pat into sides and bottom of a 9-inch non-stick pie pan. Bake at 350° F. for 10 minutes. Cool.

Filling:
¾ cup sugar
1 envelope unflavored gelatin
4 eggs, separated
⅔ cup water
¼ cup lemon juice
1 tablespoon grated lemon peel
½ teaspoon cream of tartar

Combine ½ cup of the sugar and gelatin in a small saucepan. Mix together egg yolks, water and lemon juice. Add to sugar mixture. Cook and stir over medium heat just to boiling. Remove from heat. Stir in peel. Pour into a bowl and chill until the consistency of egg whites, stirring occasionally. Beat egg whites and cream of tartar until soft peaks form. Gradually beat in remaining ¼ cup sugar, beating until stiff and glossy. Fold into chilled lemon mixture until blended and spoon into crust. Chill at least 3 hours.
Makes 6 to 8 servings.

Ricotta Rice Pudding with Lemon Sauce

A pudding to enjoy after a light supper or dinner.

2 eggs
1 cup sugar
1 cup ricotta cheese
3 tablespoons milk
1½ teaspoons grated lemon peel
3 cups cooked rice

Beat eggs and sugar together about 1 minute. Mash cheese slightly and mix with milk and lemon peel. Add to egg mixture. Beat or whirl in blender of Food Preparation System or food processor until smooth. Stir in rice. Pour into a buttered flat 5 cup (1¼-quart) baking dish. Bake at 350° F. for about 1 hour. Serve warm with lemon sauce. **Makes 6 servings.**

Lemon Sauce: Mix together ½ cup sugar, 1 tablespoon cornstarch, a dash of salt and gradually stir in 1 cup boiling water. Cook and stir about 5 minutes until sauce is thickened and clear. Stir in 1 tablespoon butter or margarine, 1 tablespoon grated lemon peel and 3 tablespoons lemon juice. Serve warm. **Makes 1⅓ cups.**

Charlotte a la Monticello

A spectacular molded dessert that tastes just as good as it looks.

1 cup orange juice
¼ cup fresh lemon juice
1 teaspoon grated lemon peel
¾ cup sugar
1 envelope unflavored gelatin
2 eggs, separated
8 to 10 lady fingers
2 cups sliced strawberries
½ cup Kirsch liqueur

Beat together orange and lemon juice and peel, ½ cup sugar, gelatin and egg yolks. Stir over low heat with a whisk until mixture thickens. Pour over stiffly beaten egg whites and set in a pan of ice water. Beat until thick enough to hold shape. Line a 5-cup (1¼-quart) mold with lady fingers and spoon orange mixture into mold. Chill until set. To serve, unmold on plate. Cut into servings and serve with sauce made by mixing 2 cups strawberries with remaining ¼ cup sugar and Kirsch. **Makes 6 servings.**

Nut Torte

This dessert can be prepared in advance. It also can be frozen. Using your Food Preparation System, whip the whites and sugar with the whisk used in the bowl at speed No. 4.

3 egg whites
1 cup sugar
½ teaspoon baking powder
1 cup fine cracker crumbs (27 single saltines, crushed)
¾ cup chopped nut meats
1 teaspoon vanilla extract
1 pint vanilla ice cream
Fruit or chocolate sauce, if desired

Beat egg whites until stiff. Mix sugar and baking powder and gradually beat into egg whites. Continue beating until egg whites hold stiff peaks. Fold in crumbs, nuts and vanilla. Pour into a lightly buttered non-stick 9-inch pie pan. Bake at 325° F. for 30 minutes.

To serve, cool completely. Cut into 6 wedges. Top each with ice cream. If desired, spoon over some fruit or chocolate sauce. **Makes 6 servings.**

Sweet Potato Pudding

This is a version of George Washington's pudding of the same name. The original called for 1 pound of butter.

1 pound of sweet potatoes
½ pound butter
1 egg
½ cup sugar
½ cup heavy cream
½ teaspoon nutmeg
¼ cup California brandy

Scrub and cook sweet potatoes in the skin in boiling salted water until tender. Peel while hot and mash with butter, beating until light and fluffy. Cool. Beat egg and sugar together and fold with remaining ingredients into cooled potatoes. Spoon into a well-buttered 4 to 5-cup (1 to 1¼-quart) casserole and bake at 375° F. for 45 minutes or until lightly browned. **Makes 6 servings.**

Note: If using the Food Preparation System, mash potatoes with the stirrer on speed No. 3 or No. 4. Cool in the bowl and add egg and sugar and continue to beat on speed No. 3 until light. Add remaining ingredients and use speed No. 1 or No. 2.

Brandy Whipped Cream Sauce

A special sauce for that Thanksgiving or Christmas pie or pudding.

1 egg
⅓ cup melted butter
1 cup sifted confectioners' sugar
Dash salt
1 tablespoon California brandy
1 cup whipping cream

Beat egg until light and fluffy. Beat in butter, sugar, salt and brandy. Whip cream until stiff and gently fold into egg mixture. Cover and chill until ready to use. Stir before using. **Makes about 3 cups.**

Note: In the Food Preparation System, beat egg, butter, sugar, salt and brandy with whisk on speed No. 4. Remove to another bowl and whip cream with whisk on speed No. 3 or No. 4.

Mint Sauce with Pears

A cool ending for a meal.

½ cup mint jelly
1 tablespoon cornstarch
⅓ cup water
1½ teaspoons grated orange peel
¼ cup créme de menthe liqueur
Dash salt
2 fresh ripe Bartlett pears
Vanilla ice cream

Melt jelly in a small saucepan. Add cornstarch to water and mix into jelly. Cook and stir until thickened. Add peel, liqueur and salt and mix well. Peel, halve and core pears. Slice each half lengthwise into 4 pieces. Stir into sauce. Serve hot or cold over ice cream. **Makes 4 servings.**

Fresh Fruit Mold

A light and pretty way to serve fruit.

1 package (4 servings) lime flavor gelatin
1 cup boiling water
½ cup cold water
2 cups diced fresh California peaches or nectarines
1 cup fresh strawberries, quartered
½ cup seedless green grapes
½ cup miniature marshmallows
1 cup whipping cream

Dissolve gelatin in boiling water. Add cold water and chill until mixture mounds on spoon. Fold fruits and marshmallows into gelatin mixture. Whip cream until stiff and fold into fruit-gelatin mixture. Spoon into a non-stick 9 x 5 x 3-inch loaf pan. Chill until firm. Slice and serve with crisp cookies. **Makes 6 to 8 servings.**

Andrea's Chocolate Velvet

Smooth and velvety with so much flavor.

1 pint whipping cream
1 can (16 ounces) chocolate syrup
4 tablespoons liqueur such as Grand Marnier or Cointreau or Créme de Cocao or Curacao

Whip cream very stiff. Fold in chocolate syrup and liqueur of your choice. Put in a plastic container, cover, and freeze several hours or overnight. Serve in your prettiest stemmed crystal dessert dishes. **Makes 6 servings.**

Tropical Fruit Squares

A cheery combination for a luncheon dessert.

1 can (21 ounces) cherry pie filling
½ cup sugar
1 can (20 ounces) crushed pineapple and juice
1 tablespoon cornstarch
Dash salt
1 package (4 servings) raspberry flavor gelatin
6 bananas, sliced
1 cup chopped pecans
Whipped topping

Combine pie filling with sugar, pineapple including juice, cornstarch and salt. Cook and stir until mixture boils and is thickened. Add gelatin and stir until dissolved. Cool, stirring occasionally. When mixture begins to thicken, stir in bananas and pecans and spoon into a non-stick 13 x 9 x 2-inch pan. Chill until firm. Cut into squares and serve with whipped topping. **Makes 12 to 16 servings.**

Indian Pudding

The slow cooker is ideal for cooking this famous New England dessert.

1 can (13 ounces) evaporated milk
1 quart whole or skim milk
1 cup yellow corn meal
½ cup dark molasses
¼ cup granulated sugar
¼ cup butter or margarine
¼ teaspoon salt
¼ teaspoon baking soda
2 eggs
1½ pints vanilla ice cream

Combine milks and heat 3 cups in the cooker pot. When milk is hot, stir in corn meal, molasses, sugar, butter, salt, baking soda and eggs with a whisk. Continue stirring with the whisk until mixture comes to a boil. Using hot pads, transfer to heating base. Heat remaining 3 cups milk and stir into corn meal mixture until well blended. Cover. Set at No. 3 and cook for 6 hours. Remove cover and stir pudding up from the bottom about 3 or 4 times during the cooking. Serve hot with vanilla ice cream. **Makes about 8 servings.**

Bread and Butter Pudding

A dessert to serve when the rest of the menu is light.

3 slices buttered white bread
3 cups whole milk
½ cup sugar
1 teaspoon vanilla extract
4 eggs, slightly beaten
¼ cup raisins
Nutmeg, if desired

Cut bread into cubes and mix with milk, sugar, vanilla, eggs and raisins. Spoon into a buttered 6-cup (1½-quart) casserole. Sprinkle with nutmeg, if desired. Place casserole in a hot water bath and bake at 325° F. for about 40 minutes or until custard is set. **Makes 6 servings.**

Coffee Fluff

A lovely ending.

1 pound marshmallows
½ cup strong coffee
1 teaspoon vanilla extract
½ cup chopped pecans
1 pint whipped cream

In the top of a double boiler melt marshmallows in coffee over boiling water. When marshmallows are melted, transfer mixture to a bowl and chill in the refrigerator until it begins to thicken. Fold in vanilla, pecans and whipped cream. Chill until firm. Serve in your prettiest goblet. **Makes 6 servings.**

Jelly Crêpes

These simple crêpes can be the base for a last minute dessert.

2 eggs, well beaten
⅔ cup milk
1 tablespoon vegetable oil
¼ teaspoon salt
½ cup all-purpose flour
½ cup jelly
Confectioners' sugar, if desired

Mix together eggs, milk, vegetable oil, salt and flour. Heat a small sauté or crêpe pan to moderately hot and grease lightly. Pour about 2 tablespoons of batter in pan and tip pan to make a pancake about 4 to 5-inches in diameter. Cook until lightly browned, turning to brown both sides, about 3 minutes in all. Keep hot on a rack in a warm oven. When all pancakes are cooked, spread with jelly and roll. If desired, sprinkle with confectioner's sugar. **Makes 4 to 5 servings.**

Diamond Doughnuts

Served hot, these diamond shaped little doughnuts are really super.

2 cups all-purpose flour
½ teaspoon salt
1 teaspoon baking powder
½ teaspoon baking soda
1 cup milk
Oil for frying
Confectioners' sugar, granulated sugar or cinnamon sugar

Mix flour, salt, baking powder and soda. Stir in milk. Roll out to ½-inch thickness on a lightly floured board and cut into diamond shapes about 1½-inches long.

Heat 1-inch oil in electric skillet to 375° F. and fry until golden brown, turning, if necessary to brown both sides. Remove from oil, drain on absorbent toweling, and roll in sugar while still warm. **Makes about 2 dozen.**

Note: For more flavor, add ¼ teaspoon nutmeg to batter.

Chapter 11

Sips and Snacks

And now, to end our collection of Wonderful Ways with Food recipes, we offer ideas for coffees, teas, punches, popcorns and candies — the "plusses" that add to our enjoyment of food — and life itself!

Intercontinental Coffees

Very often coffee is substituted for dessert and there are many ways coffee can be prepared to double as dessert.

Viennese Coffee

Prepare coffee as you always would in your favorite coffee maker. Have ready a bowl of sweetened whipped cream and a pretty shaker of grated nutmeg. As each cup of coffee is poured, add a goodly topping of whipped cream and a shake of nutmeg — and enjoy.

Irish Coffee

Another well-known beverage. In fact Irish coffee glasses or cups can be purchased if one wishes.

Use a 7-ounce goblet, prewarmed or a coffee cup. Combine ⅔ cup hot coffee, 2 teaspoons sugar and 1 jigger Irish whiskey in the cup. Stir to dissolve the sugar and blend whiskey and coffee. Top each goblet or cup with chilled whipped cream. Add it carefully so cream stays on top and do not stir after cream is added. Heartwarming! **Makes 1 serving.**

Café Diable

Café Diable as served in a restaurant has a special cup with a goblet, like pedestal and a handle. A spoon which rests across the top of the cup is also part of the equipment. Hot coffee is poured into the cup. The spoon is put in place across the top of the cup and a small cube of sugar saturated with brandy placed in the spoon, the spoon filled with brandy also. The sugar and brandy are ignited and immediately turned over into the cup. A showy way to serve after dinner coffee.

Here is a way you can make your own Café Diable at home. Mix together ½ cup sugar, 2 teaspoons grated orange peel and ½ teaspoon grated lemon peel. Keep it in a jar in the refrigerator, covered. It makes about ½ cup. To serve put 1½ teaspoons of the orange mixture and 1 tablespoon brandy in the coffee cup. Add hot coffee and stir. **This makes one serving.**

Cappuccino

Of Italian origin, it is a nice after dinner beverage.

Serve cappuccino in demi-tasse cups and use either espresso coffee brewed in your regular coffee pot or regular coffee.

Whip cream and put about a spoonful into each demi-tasse cup and add a dash of cinnamon. Pour hot coffee over cream. Serve with sugar, if one wishes.

Espresso Treat

Use your prettiest demi-tasse cups for this specialty.

Prepare strong coffee in your coffee-maker. Combine 3 cups hot espresso with 2 jiggers brandy or other favorite liqueur and ¼ cup sugar. Prepare 8 strips of orange or lemon peel. Pour espresso into demi-tasse cups and add a twist of either lemon or orange to each cup. **Makes about 8 demi-tasse servings.**

California Coffee

An interesting beverage combination to serve after dinner or at a brunch.

4 cups milk
6 tablespoons cocoa mix
1½ cups extra-strength coffee
1 cup brandy
Whipped cream

Heat milk and cocoa mix just to boiling. Add coffee and brandy and continue heating until just below the boiling point. Serve in cups with a dab of whipped cream on each. **Makes 6 servings.**

Cafe au Lait

Cafe au Lait is a marriage of hot milk and coffee which is very pleasing.

Pour equal parts of strong coffee, regular or espresso, and hot milk into a cup. Sweeten if you please. This is a delicious breakfast beverage.

Coffee Float

Coffee and ice cream for an enticing beverage.

Chill regular coffee and sweeten with a little sugar. Put a large scoop of chocolate or vanilla ice cream in a tall glass and fill with sweetened coffee. Serve with straws and long-handled spoons. **Makes 1 serving.**

Frappe

Another agreeable coffee drink.

Prepare 2 cups double-strength coffee and chill. When ready to make the frappe, pour coffee into a cocktail shaker, add crushed ice and about 3 jiggers Créme de Cacao. Shake vigorously and pour over additional crushed ice in cocktail glasses. For that extra touch, serve with short straws. **Makes 4 servings.**

Party Punches

Mock Champagne

A bubbly punch perfect for any party.

⅔ cup sugar
⅔ cup water
1 cup grapefruit juice
½ cup orange juice
3 tablespoons grenadine syrup
1 quart chilled gingerale

Stir sugar and water over low heat until sugar is dissolved. Bring to a boil. Boil 10 minutes. Cool. Add sugar syrup to grapefruit and orange juices. Chill thoroughly. Just before serving add grenadine syrup and gingerale. **Makes 1½ quarts.**

Watermelon Wine Punch

A summer special.

2 quarts seedless cubed watermelon flesh
1 cup fresh lime juice
1 cup fresh lemon juice
2 cups orange juice
1 cup sugar
1 bottle (750mL) chilled Chablis
Ice cubes

Process watermelon until mushy in food processor using steel blade. Combine with juices and sugar and stir to dissolve sugar. Chill well. When ready to serve add wine. Serve over ice cubes. **Makes about 1 gallon.**

Tasty Teas

Apple-Flavored Tea

A cool refresher.

3 cups apple cider
¼ cup honey
2 orange slices
3-inch stick cinnamon
3 cups strong tea, chilled
Ice cubes

Combine cider with honey, orange slices and cinnamon. Simmer 10 to 15 minutes. Cool and strain. Mix with tea and serve over ice cubes in tall glasses. **Makes 6 servings.**

Pineapple Tea

Hits the spot.

2 cups tea
2 cups pineapple juice
¼ cup fresh lime juice
¼ cup superfine sugar
Ice cubes
Mint sprigs

Combine tea, pineapple juice, lime juice and sugar, stirring to dissolve sugar. Chill well. Serve in tall glasses over ice cubes. Garnish with mint sprigs. **Makes 4 servings.**

Popcorn Possibilities

Popcorn is such a popular snack it was reported recently that a movie theater made more money on its popcorn than the movies it showed. Here are some ways to expand the use of popcorn.

Tex-Mex Popcorn

To the ¼ cup oil called for in the directions of your popcorn popper add ½ teaspoon chili powder and ⅛ teaspoon garlic powder. Add ½ cup popcorn and pop as directed. No need to add butter.

Variation: Put about 1 tablespoon oil in bottom of the popper. Connect to the electricity and heat ½ cup of peanuts about 3 to 4 minutes. Add to Tex-Mex popcorn.

Cheese Popcorn

Make your own.

Put popped corn in a flat baking pan and sprinkle with grated Parmesan or Romano cheese. Heat in a 350° F. oven for 15 to 20 minutes, stirring occasionally.

Popcorn Nut Crunch

Elegant crunchiness.

1⅓ cups sugar
1 cup butter
½ cup light or dark corn syrup
1 teaspoon vanilla extract
8 cups popped corn
⅔ cup toasted pecans
1⅓ cups toasted almonds

Combine sugar, butter and corn syrup in a 1½-quart saucepan. Bring to a boil over medium heat, stirring constantly. Continue boiling, stirring occasionally until mixture turns a light caramel color (290° F.). Remove from heat, stir in vanilla. Pour syrup over popcorn and nuts in a 13 x 9 x 2-inch bake pan. Toss with two large spoons until popcorn and nuts are coated. Spread out to dry. Break into pieces and store in tightly covered container or plastic bag. **Makes about 2 pounds.**

Old-fashioned Molasses Popcorn Balls

Old-time goodness from your popcorn.

2½ quarts unsalted popped corn
⅔ cup molasses
1½ cups sugar
½ cup water
1 teaspoon cider vinegar
⅛ teaspoon salt
3 tablespoons butter or margarine
Additional softened butter or margarine

Put popped corn into a large buttered bowl.

Combine molasses, sugar, water, vinegar and salt in a 2-quart sauce-pan. Cook over low heat until mixture boils. Cook without stirring to hard ball stage (270° F.) Remove from heat and stir in 3 tablespoons butter.

Pour over popcorn in bowl. Use a wooden spoon to mix well until every popcorn kernel is coated. With buttered hands shape lightly into 2½-inch balls. **Makes about 24.**

Variation:

Popcorn "popsicles." Push molasses syrup covered popcorn firmly into 5-ounce paper cups and insert a popsicle stick. Tear off paper cups to serve.

Sugar Crunch Popcorn

Sweet-coated kernels to eat with pleasure.

5½ cups freshly popped corn
1 cup salted peanuts
1½ cups light brown sugar, firmly packed
3 tablespoons butter or margarine

Put popcorn and peanuts in a large buttered bowl. Cook sugar and butter in a large skillet until melted and smooth. Pour at once over popcorn stirring to coat. **Makes 4 to 6 servings.**

Popcorn Balls

Another variation of popcorn balls. All kinds help create a festive atmosphere.

1½ quarts freshly popped corn
½ cup sugar
½ cup light corn syrup
⅛ teaspoon salt
Softened butter or margarine

Keep popped corn warm in a 275° F. oven.

Combine sugar, syrup and salt in a 2-quart saucepan. Cook and stir over medium low heat until mixture boils. Cook without stirring 4 minutes. Remove from heat and pour slowly over the popped corn mixing with a wooden spoon. When cool enough to handle, but still quite warm, grease hands with butter and shape into 2½-inch balls. Makes about 8 to 10 servings.

Variations:
Chocolate popcorn balls: Add ½ cups chocolate chips to syrup.
Tinted balls: At Christmas time or other special occasions, add food coloring indicative of the season to the syrup before adding it to the popcorn.

Popcorn Honey Cake

One more way to dress up popcorn.

3 quarts freshly popped corn
1 cup honey
1 cup sugar
⅛ teaspoon salt
Put the popcorn in a large buttered bowl.

Boil together honey, sugar and salt until syrup reaches firm ball stage, 245° F. Pour over popcorn in a thin stream, mixing with a wooden spoon as you pour. Press popcorn into a buttered non-stick 13 x 9 x 2-inch pan and let cool. Cut into squares. **Makes 24 servings.**

Dandy Candies

Butter Toffee

For that sweet tooth.

1 cup butter
1 cup sugar
¼ cup water
½ teaspoon salt
1 cup chocolate chips

Combine butter, sugar, water and salt in a saucepan. Cook, stirring constantly, to hard crack stage (300° F.) watching carefully. Immediately pour into an ungreased 13 x 9 x 2-inch pan. Cool until hard. Melt chocolate chips and spread on toffee. Let chocolate set for 2 to 3 hours and break candy into bite-size pieces. **Makes about ½ pound.**

Candied Walnuts

A sweet delicacy to please your favorite people.

1 cup sugar
¼ cup light corn syrup
⅓ cup water
1 teaspoon rum extract
⅛ teaspoon salt
2 cups walnut pieces

Combine sugar, corn syrup and water in a 2-quart saucepan. Stirring constantly, cook over medium heat until sugar is dissolved and mixture boils. Continue cooking until mixture reaches 235° F. or the soft ball stage. Stir occasionally. Remove from heat. Add rum extract, salt and walnuts. Stir until mixture begins to thicken and turn white. Pour onto a well-buttered baking sheet. Using two forks, separate into clusters. Cool and store in an air tight container. **Makes 1 pound.**

Chocolate Fudge

A fudge to make when time is short.

1 package (12 ounces) chocolate chips
¾ cup margarine
3 cups sugar
1 cup evaporated milk
1½ cups chopped pecans
⅛ teaspoon salt
1 teaspoon vanilla extract

Partially melt chocolate and margarine in a stainless steel mixing bowl. In a medium-size saucepan bring sugar and evaporated milk to a full rolling boil, stirring constantly. Pour over chocolate-butter mixture. Add pecans, salt and vanilla. Stir until creamy. Pour into a buttered 8 or 9-inch baking pan. Chill 2 to 3 hours. Cut into squares. **Makes about 3 pound(s).**

Maple Walnut Fudge

A great taste from Vermont.

2 cups maple syrup
1 tablespoon light corn syrup
½ cup milk
¼ cup cream
⅛ teaspoon salt
½ cup coarsely chopped walnuts

Combine syrups, milk, cream and salt in a 2-quart saucepan. Place over low heat and stir until mixture begins to boil.

Cook without stirring to 235° F., or the soft ball stage. Remove from heat and cool to 110° F., lukewarm, without stirring. Beat until fudge is creamy and loses gloss. Add nuts and spoon into a greased shallow pan. When firm, cut into squares. **Makes about 1¼ pounds.**

Index

Index

Index

Index